PRAISE

Flying with a Dragon on Our Tail

"I have known Jim and Judy for many years but never knew the details of the air races they flew in. It is no surprise to me, though. Judy is never one to shy away from a challenge and is always looking for the next adventure. Jim and Judy have always been generous within their community, and it is wonderful to see their spirit shine through on the pages of this book."

—U.S. SENATOR DIANNE FEINSTEIN

"The only part of this book you can take exception to is the opening sentence where Jim and Judy are described as a 'perfectly normal husband and wife.' They're anything but. They're exceptional! Race director Bernard Lamy described his race participants as 'crazy but not foolish,' but life begins at the end of your comfort zone, and whilst it's scary to step out, doing so with the correct training, guidance, and company is a recipe for amazing adventure. Richard Burton wrote, 'The gladdest moment in human life is a departure into unknown lands'—cue Paris-Pékin-Paris 1987."

—STEPHEN BEECHCROFT-KAY
   Training Captain, British Airways Boeing 787 Fleet
   Round-the World Air Race Participant, 1992

"Based on my thirty-five years of worldwide international flying with Pan Am and United, it's a heartfelt joy to realize that these dear friends of mine had even contemplated such a perilous adventure. I know the dangers of frigid open ocean waters. During my USAF years I flew fighters over the Bering Sea. To even attempt a flight such as this at any time of the year requires a very large balls-to-brains ratio. My friends, the Bells, qualify in spades."

—WILLIAM JOE CONWAY, JR.
   Retired USAF Fighter Squadron Commander;
   Captain Pan Am and United Airlines (ret)

"For a race experience that's thirty-three years in the past, this story still packs a wallop of excitement. Judy and Jim literally flew into the unknown and came out of it with great stories to tell."

—JACQUELINE B. BOYD, PHD
   Winged Women's Words

"It's empowering and exhilarating to read of Judy's adventurous spirit as she confronts real danger with incredible courage and determination."

—PAMELA WALLACE
   Academy Award–winning screenwriter of the film *Witness*

"Having flown many air races myself in the seventies and eighties, including the Powder Puff Derby in 1976, I know the challenges involved. To even consider flying a single-engine airplane in an air race from Paris to Pékin (China) and back to Paris again, is truly an unbelievable task that makes for great reading! Judy and Jim not only accomplished that amazing feat but documented the entire event in their great book Flying with a Dragon on Our Tail. Their story is truly a page-turning book, and a must-read for any pilot, or reader, who flies or desires true adventure in their lives."

—JULIE E. CLARK
   Captain, Northwest Airlines, Delta Airlines (ret)
   International Airshow Performer 1978–2019

"The thrill of flying for hours over the silent darkness of the ocean, the joy of watching the sun rise again out of cold desert sands, the desire of diving toward the fresh green of Burma's jungle—emotions that Judy and Jim make me relive intensely in the pages of this exciting adventure."

—MAURO MASON
   Captain of Italia Wings in the Paris-Pékin-Paris Air Race, 1987
   Captain, Alitalia (ret)

"This is a true and very readable story of an amazing adventure by a Fresno couple who joined an international air race not just to test themselves, but to extend Fresno's friendship to other countries. It's a story of how to meet challenges—some unanticipated—and to persevere when good sense tells you to turn back. Jim Bell and Judy Lund-Bell made Fresno proud of them as pilots, as adventurers, and as ambassadors for the community they love. They did it all over again (and then some) in 1992—all the way around the world! It was exciting to follow their exploits and it's gratifying to know them as very special people."

—KAREN HUMPHREY
former Fresno Mayor and former City Councilmember

"Mon père nous a transmis, à mon frère et à moi, la passion de voler. Il avait lui-même hérité cela de son grand-père, héros de l'aéropostale et grand ami de Jean Mermoz. Quand il nous a annoncé, à 50 ans passés, qu'il avait décidé de se lancer, à plein temps, dans l'organisation de courses d'avions légers, en lâchant son poste de directeur export, nous étions plus que perplexes.

Nous étions, avec mon frère, à l'époque jeunes copilotes sur Boeing 727 à Air France. Du temps a passé et nous sommes aujourd'hui commandant de bord sur le plus gros avion commercial du monde, l'Airbus A320.

Que de souvenirs quand j'y pense. Quelle folie s'était emparé de mon père pour imaginer cette course folle, de Paris à Pékin avec des avions légers? Qui seraient assez fous pour oser s'aventurer dans une telle épopée?

C'est à cette époque que j'ai connu Jim et Judy. Ils venaient de Californie et avaient décidé de participer à l'aventure.

Se rendaient-ils compte vraiment de l'ampleur de la tâche ? Sûrement pas, mais ils l'ont fait, et je remercie le destin de les avoir mis sur ma route, car depuis cette course folle, un lien indéfectible nous uni. Ils sont ma famille de cœur depuis plus de 30 ans maintenant. Ils ont osé, et ont réussi.

Cette épopée a changé la vie de beaucoup d'entre nous, et nous pouvons dire: « Nous y étions «. Cela nous unira à jamais, autour de la mémoire de mon père, aujourd'hui disparu, mais qui nous regarde sûrement de la haut, avec ce regard bienveillant qui le caractérisait. Je vous aime Jim et Judy pour la vie. Votre fils de cœur, Bruno."

[TRANSLATION]
"My father [Bernard Lamy, race director] passed on to my brother and me the passion of flying. He had himself inherited this passion from his grandfather, a hero of Aéropostale and great friend of Jean Mermoz. When he

announced to us, at the age of fifty, that he had decided to launch himself, fulltime, into the organizing of light air races, leaving his position as export director, we were more than perplexed.

At that time, my brother and I were young copilots on the Air France Boeing 727. Time went by, and today we are commanders of the biggest commercial airplane in the world, the Airbus A320.

So many memories when I think of it. What madness possessed my father to imagine that crazy race, from Paris to Peking with light airplanes? Who would be crazy enough to dare such an epic adventure? It is at this time that I met Jim and Judy. They came from California and had decided to participate in this adventure. Were they really aware of its monumental task? Certainly not, but they did it, and I thank fate for having put them on my path, because since this crazy race, an unbreakable bond unites us. They have been my loving family for over thirty years now.

They dared to succeed. That epic has changed the lives of many among us, and we can say 'We did it.' This will unite us forever, around my father's memory, who has now passed away, but who is surely watching us from above, with the characteristic kind look of his. I love you, Jim and Judy, for life. Your loving son, Bruno."

—BRUNO LAMY
Captain, Air France A320

Flying

WITH A

DRAGON

ON OUR TAIL

in the Historic 1987

Paris-Pékin-Paris

Air Race

JUDY LUND-BELL & JIM BELL

Published by
LundBell Books LLC
www.TheFlyingBells.com

ISBN (paperback): 978-1-7356566-1-8
ISBN (ebook): 978-1-7356566-2-5
ISBN (audiobook): 978-1-7356566-3-2

Image credits: The Paris-Pekin-Paris logo is used with the permission of Arc en Ciel. Photos on pages 48, 63, 155, 184 (top), and 199, are used with permission, © REZA. Photos on pages 29, 41, 42 (top), 44 (top), 52, 81, 88, 113, 118, 135, 152, 153, 157, 160, 165, and 167 courtesy of Allen Funch. Photo on page 89 courtesy of David Beechcroft-Kay. Photo on page 90 courtesy of Jean-Michel Masson. Photo on page 102 courtesy of Maurice Painchaud. Photo on page 184 (bottom) courtesy of Edward Lund. Photo on page 187 courtesy of Gretchen Rosenquist. All other photos and documents are personal photos taken by the authors and items from their archives.

To Bernard Lamy

who changed our lives.

Contents

Introduction

Cloud cover obscured the light from the moon and stars above, and there were no lights on the ground beneath us. As we flew our single-engine Cessna T210 through the dark night about 120 nautical miles south of Beijing, our engine coughed, sputtered, and choked.

The sound sharply intruded on our peaceful flight, as our engine was no longer purring along reassuringly as usual. It continued to run, but it was running rough and misfiring severely enough that we thought it might stop at any moment.

Our radios were silent. We were no longer in radio contact with Wuhan, and we were not yet in radio contact with Beijing. No navigational aids were operating in this part of China, so we were flying with only a watch and a compass to guide us.

It was impossible to know the terrain beneath us. If it was flat and level, we could land, even in the dark. That would take skill as well as luck, and I was glad that my husband, Jim, was flying this leg and not me, as his landing skills were superior to mine.

If we were flying over hills, a lake, or a forest, it would be difficult or impossible to land safely. Since no one knew our location, we may not be found quickly, if ever. Jim and I agreed that the worst possible scenario would be to land in a village or inhabited area, destroying homes and injuring people.

Both of us remained calm. We agreed that, even if the worst happened, we were having a great adventure flying in the historic 1987 Paris-Pékin-Paris Air Race with the organization's dragon logo on our tail and following our dreams.

I turned to Jim in the pilot seat and said, "We knew when we decided to do this that there would be risks."

"Crashing in China at midnight was not something we contemplated," he said with unusual calm and then suggested, "We could be home watching TV and going to bed early."

I took a deep breath and replied, "We wanted to have an adventure. Sometimes there is a price to pay."

Jim nodded his head in agreement. "It is better to live life fully and taste all of its incredible flavors."

"I hope that this will not be a bitter one," I said and studied the chart on my lap.

Jim concentrated on the sounds emanating from the engine as though willing it with his mind to continue running. I did not want Jim to see the tears that filled my eyes when I thought of our children. Flying this air race was our decision, and we had chosen to assume the risks. They had not. They would not only miss us, they would be devastated if we crashed and died in a remote area of China.

I wished I could tell them again how much I love them. Our future grandchildren would never know us or we them. I could not express my feelings to Jim now, as he needed to concentrate on keeping the airplane in the air, so I remained silent.

We are writing this book and you are reading it, so we obviously survived. Our sputtering engine got us safely through the dark night and back on the ground in China. And we finished the race in Paris with enough memories and stories to fill a book.

Jim and I each logged about 300 pages of our memories from the air race and all of our exotic destinations as soon as we returned home from the race. My notes and observations were more personal. Jim's reflected more the logistical side of the routes. And now, more than thirty years after this daring adventure, I have combined our notes and memories to tell about flying with a dragon on our tail in this once-in-a-lifetime event.

I thought back to the time when we first learned of this air race and decided to join sixteen other airplanes in a flight from Paris, France, to Beijing, China, and back. Why did we not give more thought to the risks that might be involved? Did we assume that we were invincible and could overcome any obstacles? How did two lawyers from Fresno, California, husband and wife, arrive at the decision to fly our small airplane halfway across the world?

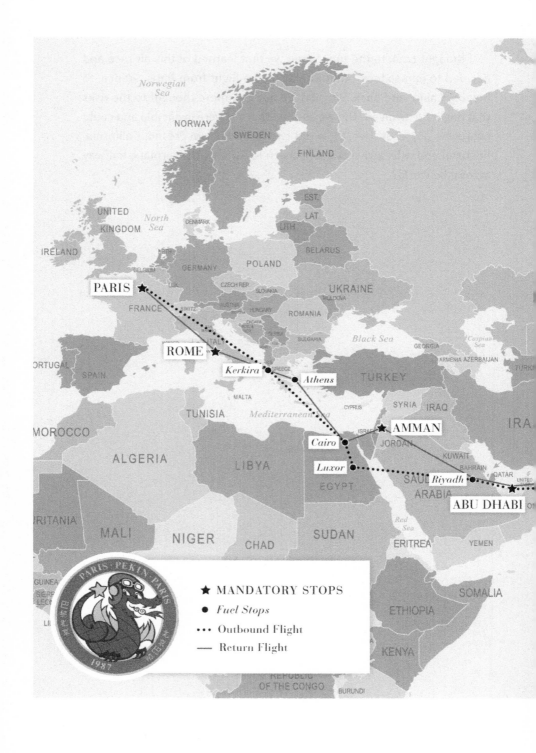

Norwegian
Sea

NORWAY
SWEDEN
FINLAND

UNITED *North
KINGDOM Sea* DENMARK
IRELAND
BELGIUM
GERMANY POLAND
PARIS ★
FRANCE SWITZ. UKRAINE
CZECH REP.
SLOVAKIA
ROMANIA
CROATIA HUNGARY
Black Sea
ROME ★
BULGARIA GEORGIA *Caspian Sea*
PORTUGAL *Kerkira* GREECE ARMENIA AZERBAIJAN TURK
Athens TURKEY
SPAIN
MALTA
TUNISIA *Mediterranean Sea* CYPRUS SYRIA IRAQ
MOROCCO ISRAEL ★ AMMAN IRA
Cairo JORDAN
ALGERIA LIBYA *Luxor* KUWAIT
SAUDI *Riyadh* BAHRAIN
EGYPT QATAR UNITED
ARABIA ★ ABU DHABI O
MAURITANIA *Red Sea*
MALI NIGER
CHAD SUDAN ERITREA YEMEN

GUINEA
SIERRA
LEONE SOMALIA
LIB
ETHIOPIA

KENYA
REPUBLIC
OF THE CONGO
BURUNDI

★ MANDATORY STOPS
● *Fuel Stops*
••• Outbound Flight
— Return Flight

PARIS · PEKIN · PARIS
1987

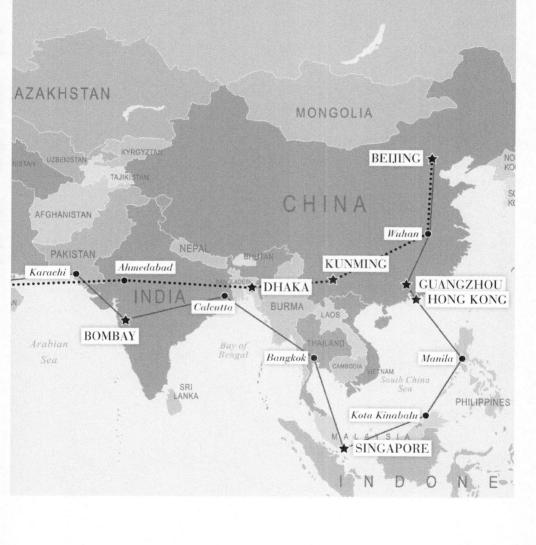

THE FLIGHT OF
Winged Quest

1

Fresno, California: Making the Decision

Fall 1986

Why would a perfectly normal husband and wife in their forties agree to fly an unpressurized single-engine airplane in an international air race from Paris to Beijing and back—a distance of approximately 20,000 nautical miles?

Jim and I had shared a passion for flying since we were young. He had flown with a family friend in Arkansas when he was about two years old and had wanted to become a pilot since then. He joined the Air Force hoping to fly, but they did not need pilots at that time, so he resigned and went to law school at UC Berkeley. After he became an attorney and joined a law firm in Fresno, California, he eagerly began taking flying lessons and obtained his pilot's license in 1973.

I was hooked after watching airplanes take off and land at the Phoenix airport when I was in the sixth grade. I still remember the feeling of awe, standing with my fingers interlocked in a chain-link fence and watching the graceful airplanes ascend into the beautiful blue sky and fly away where I could no longer see them. Sometimes they flew into a puffy cloud.

I had no idea how I would do this, but I wanted to fly someday—and knew I would. I was divorced with two children when I attended San Joaquin College of Law in Fresno full-time and worked twenty to thirty hours a week to support us. When I completed law school, no firms were hiring women, so I opened my own practice in a windowless storeroom of an attorney whom I had worked for as a law clerk. Within six months I was busy enough to move into an office with four other solo practitioners. Then, in 1980, I paid for flying lessons and obtained my pilot's license with my first discretionary income.

By the time we decided to fly the air race, Jim and I had been married for five years—second marriages for us—and we each brought two children to our family. In addition to our private pilot's licenses, we both had obtained our instrument rating, which meant that we could fly when we could not visually see our surroundings. Flying was not simply a means for traveling from one place to another for us. It was a shared passion.

Jim had been reading *Flying* magazine, and a small article caught his attention, which he read aloud to me. It announced an airplane race, "The Paris-Pékin-Paris Air Race," sponsored by Arc en Ciel, a French organization. (*Pékin* is the French word for Peking, or what is now Beijing. Technically there is an accent over the e, but in the official name of the race it was omitted.)

"For more information, contact Marc Mosier at a post office box in New York," the article said. We were curious, so we sent for more information. In response, we received a letter from Marc, requesting $60 (nonrefundable) in order to receive the General Regulations, an information kit, and a registration form. We were to make the check payable to him personally.

We hesitated. Why was the check to be payable to him personally and not to the organization? Could this be a scam? We thought that it probably was not, as he would have asked for more money.

"Can you even imagine flying from Paris to Beijing, China?" we wondered.

"We have flown all around the US," Jim said.

"Yes, and also to Baja California in Mexico and to the Bahamas," I added.

Smiling, we thought of our many wonderful flights to distant places around the United States and Mexico. But France, China, and all the countries between? What would the route be? Probably not a straight line and probably not north, as it would be February, and it would be cold with snowstorms. How would this work? We couldn't fly over the Middle East, could we?

We were both curious and not sold on flying through such unknown lands, but we each fed off the other's enthusiasm and did not want to appear to be less adventurous than the other. It was almost a competition between us.

Satisfying our curiosity was worth a small investment, we decided, and at this point, we had nothing to lose other than our $60. I wrote the check, and Jim addressed the envelope. On August 10, 1986, we sent off the money to an unknown person at a post office box across the country for information on a crazy adventure with minimal expectation that we would do more than simply review the information—if we even received a response.

We were pleasantly surprised when we soon received the complete rules that set out the requirements and necessary qualifications for the crew. The race was to begin on February 28, 1987, in Paris, and return on March 28 to Paris (later changed to March 27, 1987). The route would take us over mountains (Alps and Himalayas), water (Mediterranean Sea, Gulf of Oman, South China Sea, and other bodies of water), deserts (Sinai), and jungles (Burma and China).

If we had an engine failure over any of these hazardous places, we may not survive. This incredible adventure, which had been simply a curiosity, suddenly became real. We still were not sold, but we continued to take steps to learn more. We told each other that staying in the loop was simply to quell our curiosity, not that we would actually do it, and agreed that taking a few steps at this point would not really be a commitment.

We had been curious about the route, and now found that once the race began in Paris, there would be mandatory stops for between two to four days in Abu Dhabi, United Arab Emirates; Dhaka, Bangladesh; Kunming, China, to clear customs; Beijing, China; Guangzhou, China (overnight);

Hong Kong; Singapore; Bombay, India; Amman, Jordan; Rome, Italy; and back to Paris.

The rules provided information as to how the winner would be selected, as follows:

> *The winning crew will be the one flying his aircraft with the best ratio between his ground speed (Vs) and his True Air Speed (Vp) taken at 65% of max power, at optimum altitude. Each crew will race against the clock.*
>
> *None of the aircraft have sufficient fuel to fly nonstop to the compulsory stopovers, so they will have to land at various places in between for refueling. Each crew will be responsible for mapping their route and selecting places for refueling.*
>
> *Time spent at stopovers will not be deducted for any reason. Between these stopovers, the crews will fly by night and day, navigating as best as they can.*

The rules contained another unusual twist. Each crew would be composed of not only two pilots but also a photojournalist who would document the flight. We discussed many well-qualified candidates and rejected them for one reason or another, until we focused on one obvious candidate: Allen Funch.

Allen was an avid photographer who owned a shopping center and had the time to participate. We took Allen to lunch to discuss the race. Allen said, "I have a passport. My bags are packed. Let's go!" We had found our photojournalist and had taken another step.

Cooking is another of my passions, and I had planned a trip to Westport, Connecticut, in October of 1986 for a weeklong cooking class with Martha Stewart. It was a wonderful week, and my days were consumed with learning about herbs, cooking and preparation techniques, decorating, and all that Martha had to teach us.

One day, she invited us to her home where we strolled through her gardens, talked to her chickens, and saw where she actually entertained. It was a fantastic week, and flying to China could not have been further from my mind.

Jim stayed in California, and even though we had made no decisions, he began researching everything that we would need to do and acquire to prepare our airplane—just in case we decided to fly the race. Another step.

Since I was on the East Coast, Jim and I decided that I should stop in New York to check out Marc Mosier to see if he was legitimate. I arrived unannounced at the French bank where he worked, half expecting him to not exist. He was surprised to see me, but invited me to lunch. I had arrived just before lunchtime, because I assumed that he would take a break from work and I could speak with him. I did not expect to be fed.

We talked throughout lunch, and he gave me much more information about the organization, the people involved, as well as the race itself. He passed the initial test: he not only existed, but he paid for lunch.

Not long afterward, Jim and I were in Los Angeles at a time when Marc was there as well. We had a lengthy dinner together, and he impressed both of us. He explained that the race director, Bernard Lamy, had organized two previous air races, one from Paris to Marrakesh and the other from France to Saint-Louis du Sénégal and on to Brazil to commemorate the fiftieth anniversary of the Aéropostale pilots who had flown the mail across the South Atlantic in the 1930s.

The more we talked, the more we became interested in what would be a historic flight from Paris to Beijing and back. It almost felt as though we were joining those brave Aéropostale pilots like Antoine de Saint-Exupéry that we had only read about. He had written one of my favorite books, *Le Petit Prince* (*The Little Prince*). What a thrill it would be to have an actual connection to him.

> **JIM'S NOTES:** *After we met with Marc in LA, we decided to prepare the airplane, just in case we decided to participate in the race.*
>
> *The firm decision to participate had come so late that serious problems developed in preparing the aircraft. We decided to install Flint Aero tip tanks, a satellite navigation system (Sat Nav) an Arnav Loran, a stormscope (borrowed from a friend), and an HF radio (again borrowed). However, there was only about one month to accomplish all of these tasks. The tip tank modification required FAA approval (called STC). Such approval usually took months,*

*but we hoped to obtain the approval and have all of the avionics
modifications installed in one month.*

*I flew the airplane to San Diego for the tip tank installation.
After about two weeks, the aircraft was returned with the tip tanks
installed. We were informed that the paperwork would follow and
that at least, in the meantime, we could have the avionics work
completed. But then there was a problem.*

*Once the aircraft had been torn up for the installation of the
avionics, a representative from Flint Aero called to report that the
FAA had made some mistakes in logging their data during the
tests of the aircraft before and after the tip tank installation, and it
was necessary to take the tip tanks off, fly the aircraft to run tests,
reinstall the tip tanks, run more tests, and thereby verify the data.
This was done at great expense to Flint Aero.*

*Finally, on Friday afternoon before the aircraft was to leave for
Paris on Monday, the STC and Air Worthiness Certificate were issued
by the FAA. The radio work was completed over the weekend, and
the aircraft was scheduled to leave for Paris on Monday, February 16.
During a test flight on Saturday, February 14, it was discovered that
the DME was operating erratically.*

The Executive Wings avionics shop worked on the aircraft on Monday, and the aircraft left on Tuesday the 17th for Paris.

We were accustomed to raising money for good causes, but for ourselves? It was a challenge to raise the money for our own adventure,
and we felt selfish asking for money. Jim was on the board of the local
Valley Children's Hospital, so we decided to take the hospital mascot,
a stuffed giraffe, with us on the air race to potentially raise money for
the hospital.

We didn't specifically discuss it, but in thinking back, supporting the
hospital helped ameliorate our guilt at raising the money simply for ourselves. It seemed less selfish to ask sponsors for money if we were flying
this race for a worthy cause.

An artist friend designed a giraffe "flying" our airplane, and we had bro-
chures printed so that people could pledge money to the hospital for each

WINGED QUEST

Fly-a-Long
on the
ARC EN CIEL   Paris · Beijing · Paris Air Race
Benefitting Valley Children's Hospital · Fresno, California
February 28, 1987 to March 28, 1987

On February 28, 1987, twenty general aviation aircraft will leave Paris, France to begin an historic international air race from Paris to Beijing, China and back to Paris. Three of these planes will be from the United States. ONE WILL BE FROM FRESNO, CALIFORNIA.

Jim Bell and Judy Lund-Bell will fly the race in a Cessna Turbo 210, Centurian with Allen Funch as the airplane's official photographer. Accompanying the trio will be a stuffed giraffe, the mascot of Valley Children's Hospital in Fresno.

This is the first time in history that the People's Republic of China has allowed general aviation aircraft to overfly its territory and land at its airfields.

YOU ARE INVITED to join Jim, Judy, Allen and the giraffe as they leave Paris, refuel at Corfu, soar across the Mediterranean to Aqaba, cross Saudi Arabia at night and land at Abu Dhabi near dawn to complete the first leg of the race. Your progress with the contestants will be documented in the local media during the month-long race.

JOIN THE ADVENTURE AND MAIL THE ATTACHED CARD WITH YOUR CONTRIBUTION TODAY. ALL PROCEEDS WILL BENEFIT VALLEY CHILDREN'S HOSPITAL.

ARC EN CIEL   Paris · Beijing · Paris Air Race
I want to fly-a-long to benefit Valley Children's Hospital.

I pledge:

- ☐ LEG 1 $ 5.
- ☐ LEG 2 $ 10.
- ☐ LEG 3 $ 25.
- ☐ LEG 4 $ 35.
- ☐ LEG 5 $ 50.
- ☐ LEG 6 $ 75.
- ☐ LEG 7 $100.
- ☐ LEG 8 $200.
- ☐ LEG 9 $_____
  ENTIRE RACE. WOW!

Name _____

Address _____

_____

Telephone _____

☐ Check enclosed now — I'm optimistic!
☐ I will send money at conclusion of the race.

*Make checks payable to Valley Children's Hospital Foundation.
All proceeds to benefit Valley Children's Hospital.*

Brochure we printed to request pledges in support of
Valley Children's Hospital and our fund-raising flight.

leg we completed. With the help of friends, we obtained sponsors and sufficient (just barely) funds came in. Soon our airplane was decorated nose to tail with stickers with the names and/or logos of our sponsors. Every time a sticker was added, we became more and more excited, and the adventure seemed more real. We named our airplane *Winged Quest,* so the name and a sticker with the flying giraffe's picture also were added to the airplane. He was now a part of our crew.

We had thought of many possible names for our airplane, such as *Dream Flight, Voyageur de l'Air, Wanderin' Wings, Belle Aero, La Belle Express, Aero Bell* and many, many others, but we liked the word *quest,* which reminded us of knights of old traveling far and wide and searching for something. We would certainly be traveling far and wide. Our search was not for something tangible. Rather, we were following our dreams of adventure, so the name of our airplane became *Winged Quest.*

February 1987
FERRY FLIGHT—FRESNO TO PARIS

Jim and I were required to be in Paris a week prior to the beginning of the race for briefings, so we hired an experienced ferry pilot to fly our airplane to Paris while we, along with Allen, took a commercial flight. Jim and I would both have to take time from our busy law practices and decided that it would save us a week or ten days to hire a ferry pilot. Besides, it would be another challenge to fly the North Atlantic, which we had never done, in the winter. Better to save our challenges for the air race.

On February 17, 1987, our airplane, now dubbed *Winged Quest,* an unpressurized Cessna T210, tail number N6113U, departed Fresno Air Terminal in California for Toussus-le-Noble, an airport just south of Paris, France.

The ferry pilot was Richard (Dick) Smith of Fresno, and he was accompanied by Alain Alherbe, one of my clients, also a pilot, who was born in Paris but now living in Fresno. Jim went to the airport to see them off at 8:00 a.m. local time and came home smiling, "They're off!" We were both excited, as this was the first tangible step, other than preparing our airplane, toward the actual commencement of the race.

Dick was an experienced Atlantic ferry pilot, having crossed the North Atlantic thirty-six times. However, this was his first experience with a single-engine crossing. To top it off, we were asking him to ferry a single-engine airplane to Paris during the winter without deicing or anti-icing capabilities (except the hot prop, stall horn, and pitot tube).

Ice forms when the temperature is 32 degrees Fahrenheit and the air is moist, such as in a cloud. It forms on the leading edges of the airplane (wings and tail, for example) and immediately causes a loss of efficiency. The airplane becomes heavier as more ice accumulates, which can cause it to be unable to maintain altitude.

Falling out of the sky is not a desired outcome! The remedy is to have deicing equipment, which our Cessna did not have, or to climb higher so that ice would hopefully fall off or descend lower into warmer temperatures so the ice could melt.

Dick said that he could do it. We were hopeful that he could, and were happy that we had elected not to try it ourselves. He was much braver than we were, and, of course, he had flown the North Atlantic and would be familiar with the route. This flight would be challenging, but perhaps there is something about pilots—we like challenges.

In Moncton, New Brunswick, Canada, Dick cleared customs and had the airplane inspected for the Atlantic crossing by Canadian aviation authorities. All single-engine aircraft making the crossing must be inspected, although twin-engine aircraft are exempt.

During the inspection, the inspector asked Dick to turn on the high frequency radio (HF), which he did. When the light came on in the radio, the inspector said, "Good! Some guys come through here with these things in the airplane disconnected. Can you believe that?"

Dick answered, "You're kidding me!"

What the inspector did not know is that Dick had no intention of using the HF because it pulled too much power. With the HF in use, it was necessary to turn off all the other navigation equipment. Although we were required to have one, the HF radio was never used during either the ferry flight over or back or at any time during the air race.

Dick did not know enough about the radio to use it anyway, so it is fortunate that he was not asked to transmit or receive. We had received minimal instruction on the use of the HF radio, so we would have had the same problem.

After the inspection, Dick flew the airplane to Goose Bay, Labrador, which is part of the province of Newfoundland, Canada. He landed at night in a blinding snowstorm. In the course of the instrument approach, Dick turned on the landing lights, which revealed that the aircraft was in such terrible weather conditions that forward visibility was impossible.

He quickly turned the lights off. Alain asked, "Why did you turn off the lights?"

Dick responded, "It's too scary. I'd rather not see where we are going!" When they safely landed, he and Alain checked into the so-called Goose Bay Hilton, which provides basic accommodations.

After a four-day stay in Goose Bay due to weather, Dick and Alain took off for Soderstrum, Greenland, as Dick had obtained permission to land at the US Air Force base situated there. They next flew across Greenland and the Denmark Strait to Iceland. They remained overnight and departed the next day for Prestwick, Scotland, where they also spent the night. The following day, they flew across England and the English Channel to Paris. Although this usually would be a beautiful and scenic route, the weather was too bad for sightseeing.

On Saturday, February 21, the day that Jim, Allen, and I departed for Paris, the sky was a soft, gray wash over blue like a Chinese watercolor. A friend had given us flowers and balloons, which we took with us on our flight to Los Angeles.

Not knowing what to expect, we had substantially overpacked and had quite a bit of carry-on luggage in addition to the several pieces of luggage we checked. We also were carrying a lot of cash with us, as we had been requested to pay the entry fee in US dollars and knew that we would need cash to pay for fuel along the way as well.

Since the balloons had been difficult to manage in the airplane from Fresno to Los Angeles, we reluctantly left them in the LA airport terminal connection tunnel. I did not want to leave them, as they were a tangible piece of home, but we had other things to think about and to carry, so it did not make sense to take them on the commercial flight to Paris. I could not part with the beautiful flowers, so we took them with us. Of course, they were dead when we arrived. One less thing to carry.

With all the money we were spending, we had decided that we should forgo the luxury of flying business class to Paris. However, Air France had mistakenly put us in the smoking section, which existed at that time, so we were moved to business class. It made us feel special to sit in business class with flowers.

2

Race Preparation:
Paris

I had been to Paris once, in 1973, on a "30 Days in Europe for $500" trip, and Jim had never been there, so we had no idea where to stay. We definitely did not want to share a bathroom as I had done in 1973.

The Ritz and the Hôtel de Crillon, a luxury five-star hotel on the Place de la Concorde, were both highly recommended, and we chose the Crillon, as it was slightly less expensive, but still costly. At least we knew that it had a private bath. It was marble with chandeliers, and a big improvement over those I encountered in 1973.

Security was tight throughout the city, as a trial for the Jackal, a well-known international terrorist and assassin, was in progress, and there was concern that there might be repercussions. Would we possibly be witness to some international intrigue?

The American Embassy adjacent to our hotel was heavily guarded, and the guard blew his whistle and shook his finger when Jim started to take a picture. It was exciting to know that a real terrorist that we had read about was being brought to justice nearby, but we hoped that anticipated repercussions, whatever they may be, would not impact us.

Monday, February 23, 1987

Bernard Lamy, the air race director, had been immersed in aviation since childhood, as his grandfather was an administrator of Aéropostale, which flew the mail route from France across the South Atlantic to Brazil in the 1930s. The race sponsor, Arc en Ciel (the French word for *rainbow*), was named after the first airplane to fly this route.

Bernard had always been fascinated by airplanes and flying and became a pilot himself. As a young man, he joined the French Air Force and, along with two other French pilots, attended cadet training at Hondo Air Base in Texas. He subsequently worked for Tefal, a French cookware manufacturer, flying throughout the Middle East selling cookware. His contacts from that time were important in planning this race.

Bernard, along with Gérard Emler—whose father was one of the first pilots for Aéropostale—formed the idea for the Paris-Pékin-Paris Air Race in 1985. Bernard worked on it tirelessly, planning routes and organizing hotels, meals, press conferences, and activities at the mandatory stops; obtaining permission to overfly various countries; and overcoming incredible obstacles. His wonderful wife, Maryse, shared his passion and worked with him in every venue, making all of the detailed arrangements that were necessary to house, feed, and entertain all of us. Gérard provided many contacts and financial support.

In the morning, Jim, Allen, and I went to Bernard's apartment near the Madeleine and met him, Maryse, and their son Bruno. Bernard gave us instructions for obtaining our Chinese visa, which, at that time, could not be obtained in the United States.

We went to the Chinese Embassy in the afternoon, and the staff was cooperative and processed the visas (which usually takes two to three days) for us in two and a half hours. We suffered from jet lag, and I unceremoniously fell asleep in the embassy waiting room. A friendly young lady from Brittany assisted tremendously. Jim and I had forgotten to obtain passport pictures, so she took us to a quick-photo booth in the Metro station and helped us change our money into francs and get pictures made. Actually, we did not forget. We had not even thought about it.

Wednesday, February 25, 1987

As it turned out, it had been a fortuitous decision to hire a ferry pilot to bring the airplane to Paris. Dick and Alain had left a week before we did and did not arrive in Paris until the day before the race airplanes had to be placed in impound—two days before the start of the race. We had become quite concerned, as we would not be able to participate in the race if our airplane did not arrive, and it would be a big letdown for our friends and sponsors. We thought that our giraffe would be sad also, as it could not help us raise money for Valley Children's Hospital.

Our airplane, *Winged Quest,* arrived at Toussus-le-Noble airport, just south of Paris, about noon. Jim, Allen, and I went to the airport to meet Dick and Alain. We were excited to see our airplane on French soil. Over lunch, the ferry pilots related their story of the flight over the North Atlantic in an unpressurized aircraft that was not equipped with deicing or anti-icing equipment.

Thursday, February 26, 1987

Jim and Allen were both sick. Allen had the flu, so we called a doctor for him. I was concerned, as this could definitely impact our participation in the race. Jim did not feel quite so bad and was well enough that we could attend the first race briefing at the office of the Aéroclub de France in the morning.

Professional pilots headed most of the other teams, and we wondered whether our limited flying experience was sufficient for what now seemed a formidable flight. Of course we can do it, we thought, even though it was intimidating. Flying is flying! At the briefing, Bernard told us that he would send someone to our hotel to pick up the race entry fee, which he had asked us to bring in cash: $17,250 US dollars.

We had placed the cash in a hotel security box when we arrived. Shortly after we returned to the hotel after the briefing, the front desk rang our room and told us that someone was there to see us. I assumed that Bernard would come to get the money himself, as this would be important for him.

I went downstairs and met a man who introduced himself as Gaston, whom I had never seen before, and who told me that he was there to fetch the money. My initial thought was who are you, and you want me to give you what?

I questioned him to establish, as well as possible, that he was legitimate, and then he went with me into a small room where the security boxes were located. A young lady was seated at a desk, working, and she did not leave when the security box was removed. However, as I began counting out the cash for Gaston, she got up and quickly left, evidently believing that she was witnessing something illegal. It crossed my mind that she might have thought that we were part of a plot to spring the Jackal or something equally nefarious.

I requested a receipt, and when the one produced by Gaston did not look sufficiently complete, I wrote another myself, which Gaston signed. It seemed weird to hand over that much money in cash to a stranger. It was much more serious than sending $60 to a post office box in New York. Fortunately, Gaston also was legitimate.

Friday, February 27, 1987

We moved from the luxurious Hôtel de Crillon to Hôtel le Versailles in Versailles, closer to the airport. It was different, though it still had a private bathroom, albeit a small one, with one ceiling light.

We checked in and immediately went to Toussus-le-Noble to complete final race preparations and receive our official race jacket and vest. The heavy jacket was quite warm. The vest was lightweight. Both were red and decorated with the race logo and logos of the race sponsors. We proudly put them on, smiling and posing for each other. As we looked at the other crews donning their jackets, we, for the first time, felt part of a team and had the jackets to prove it.

Dick Smith helped us apply the major race sponsors' decals (logos) to the tail surface of N6113U. These organization sponsors were Dr. Ghaith Pharaon, an investor living in Paris who was developing Mirapolis, an amusement park outside of Paris that would be the site of the awards banquet at the end of the race; Il Messaggero, the leading Italian newspaper; Internike, an insurance company; and Pilar, an investment group.

In addition to these decals, we also applied the race logo to both sides

Dick Smith, our ferry pilot, applied the colorful race logo
to the tail of our Cessna before the beginning of the race,
so we were truly flying with a dragon on our tail.

of the top of the tail. The race logo is an attractive, smiling red Chinese
dragon in a field of white, with a blue border encircling the dragon. The
words *Paris-Pekin-Paris* appear at the top of the blue border, and we were
told that the Chinese characters on each side of the dragon, also in the
blue border, said the same thing. It was a great logo and received many
favorable comments wherever we went. We loved it and thought that our
giraffe would appreciate being accompanied by a dragon. Saint-Exupéry
could have written another great story about them.

After topping our fuel tanks (main tanks and tip tanks), we taxied
the aircraft to the impound area at the base of the tower that had been
reserved for the race aircraft. It was windy, cold, and rainy, but weather
did not prevent a large crowd from arriving at the airport to see the airplanes and talk with the crews. French news reporters and camera people
surrounded the French-speaking crews and occasionally came by to

interview Jim and me as well. It felt wonderful to have so many people who were interested in what we were doing and wishing us well.

We spent the whole day there and met the other competitors. Air France, Alitalia, and Cathay Pacific captains were among the other professional pilots. Many people wanted their pictures taken with us, our airplane, and La Girafe, as he was now known by his French name.

One man who seemed interested in us and our airplane was Serge Dassault of Dassault Aviation, which builds the French Mirage. The Second Secretary from the Chinese Embassy asked to have her picture taken in our airplane, and of course we obliged and helped her into the pilot's seat. She wanted to have La Girafe in the picture, and he was pleased to comply.

At the end of the day, Bernard Lamy held the first of many briefings. Since English is the international air language, all briefings, including this first one, were conducted in English. He had a meteorologist present to discuss the weather, and he told us that the forecast was for bad weather between Paris and southern Italy. Each crew was assigned a departure time. We were scheduled to leave at 08:20 on Saturday, February 28, 1987.

The longest air race in history at that time was about to get under way.

That evening, we ate our first dinner as a group at a restaurant near the Hôtel le Versailles where we were spending our last night in the Paris area. Most of the chairs were taken when we entered the dining room, but we did manage to find empty chairs at one table that was occupied in part by some of the Chronopost crew and representatives of the sponsor. This was the only other Cessna 210 in the race, so obviously they would be a competitor.

Jim introduced himself, Allen, and me to George De Brito, who was to join the crew in Beijing and fly the Beijing-Paris return. He spoke English fluently and was very gracious. Jim then extended his hand by way of introduction across the table to another member of the Chronopost crew who simply turned away as though he failed to see or hear Jim. In all fairness to him, we later learned that he did not speak English well (or at all) and was simply shy.

3

Paris to Abu Dhabi

Saturday, February 28, 1987

Our wake-up time, 5:00 a.m., early and dark, came quickly at the Hôtel le Versailles on the morning of the start of the air race. We caught the bus for Toussus-le-Noble, where we joined our fellow competitors in the coffee shop for a last-minute briefing and updated weather information.

It was reassuring to see some now-familiar faces among the competitors. We proudly wore our red race jackets, as did all of the others, and this helped us to feel that we belonged there, as a part of the group. Everyone greeted us with, "See you next in Abu Dhabi!" The excitement was almost tangible as we looked around again at the fellow pilots with whom we would be sharing the next month's adventure.

The competitors, including Jim, were all leaving the coffee shop and going to their airplanes. Before I joined them, I located the *toilette,* which was down a dark hallway behind the kitchen, for a last pit stop before the first leg of our journey.

As I turned the knob on the door to exit the *toilette* and head to our airplane, the knob came off in my hand. I tried to reinsert it, tried to open the door without it, knocked, pounded, and yelled, but received no response. The music was playing loudly in the kitchen, so no one could hear me. I panicked. I was imprisoned in the *toilette*! I knew that the airplanes would be departing shortly and that Jim would be wondering where I was. What if our departure time came and I was still trapped?

I finally climbed up on the rather unstable basin, leaned out through a high, open transom, and peered down into the vacant hallway. I wondered whether I could crawl through the opening and drop to the floor below, but that didn't seem possible. It crossed my mind that if I fell and broke a leg, our adventure would end right there.

I called out again and again, and finally a young man came into the hallway carrying out the garbage. I called to him to get his attention, and he almost fainted. I showed him the broken handle, and he, with the assistance of two other men, came to my rescue and retrieved me from the *toilette*. I was finally able to rush out to the airplane.

The airplanes were scheduled to depart at ten-minute intervals. Jim and I finished packing (not loading) the aircraft, as we had substantially overpacked. Our suitcases were large and stuffed with every type of clothing we thought we could possibly need or want, but, obviously, this was not a normal vacation.

In addition, we had the necessary equipment, including a five-person raft, a survival bag with emergency supplies, and the additional items that we had been issued. The race organization had given us an emergency locator beacon/transmitter in a box in addition to the one we already had on board the aircraft, which had been factory installed. We could hardly stuff everything into the airplane.

The sky was low overcast, gray, and drizzling rain. Jim, Allen, and I were happy to be inside the airplane and out of the weather. I was relieved to be freed from the *toilette* before our takeoff time.

Jim had filed a flight plan the previous evening. It was an IFR (instrument flight rule) plan,[1] which would take us from Paris to Kerkira on the island of Corfu, Greece, our first refueling point. The weather en route was bad. It was raining hard and extremely cold. The freezing level was quite low. Jim knew that we had to fly above the freezing level where it

---

1. Flight Plan Route: Dijon (DIJ) via A-1 (airway) then A-1 and W28 to Saronno (SRN), which would cause us to cross a corner of Switzerland (Lake Geneva), then into Italy. We then would follow B-4 to Vicenza (VIC), B-23 to Chioggia (CHI), Ancona (ANC), Vieste (VIE), Brindisi (BRD), and then A-14 to Kerkira (KRK).

was too cold to form ice and, with this in mind, had filed for flight level 190 (19,000 feet).

To say that we were apprehensive would be an understatement, as we were both concerned about the weather. At home, it had been our usual practice to fly only when the weather was good. Our IFR flying usually consisted of occasionally shooting an instrument approach into Fresno, but it rarely consisted of prolonged IFR flight.

Jim did not necessarily follow the practice that an old pilot had related to him: "I only fly when the bluebirds fly," but his approach was similar. Our experience was about to change, we knew it, and thus our apprehension. Certainly we can do this, we thought optimistically. We were both trained for this, even though our actual experience had been minimal.

A large crowd had gathered to watch the departures. Reporters, television news correspondents, and well-wishers were everywhere, as well as the race organization personnel. Scheduled to depart at 8:20 local time, we were one of the first aircraft to take off. Promptly at 8:15, Jim called ground control and asked for permission to start the engine (a European practice that is not followed in the United States—one of many differences that we were to observe between flying in the United States and the rest of the world).

We had not started our engine and were concerned that, while waiting for permission to do so, we would run down the battery listening for the controller.

Finally, the French ground controller, in heavily accented English, approved the engine start, and we fired up our engine. We called ground control again and asked for permission to taxi, after announcing that we were IFR to Kerkira. The ground controller seemed surprised, as to him "start engine" meant "taxi." He cleared us to taxi to runway 25R. We probably should have checked out the "start engine" routine, but we had no idea that it would be different. We obviously had a lot to learn.

While going through the predeparture checklist, ground control asked if we were ready to copy the clearance. We said yes. What followed would have been comical if it was not so frustrating.

The controller tried to assign us a SID (standard instrument departure), which, in this case, was the ARSIL 4R departure. We expected a SID, but

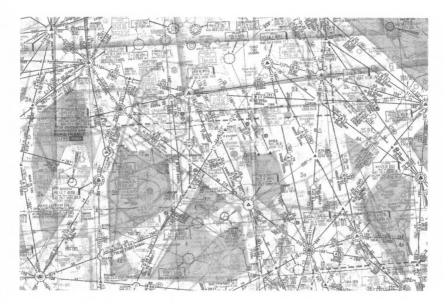

Chart of Toussus-le-Noble departure to the southeast.

did not anticipate that it would be so difficult to understand the instructions. The controller spoke English well, but we did not understand what
he was telling us and asked him to repeat the instructions several times.

The controller said that we were cleared to Dijon via the ARSIL 4R
departure, and then he gave the clearance by reference to headings and
said something about "Oscar Lima." This completely confused us. Jim
and I both searched, but we could not find Oscar Lima on either the European Low Altitude En route Chart or the Paris Area Chart.

Finally, the controller gave up and asked us to return to the ramp. We
were discouraged and embarrassed. It was our first flight in Europe, our
first departure in the Paris-Pékin-Paris Air Race, and we could not understand the controller's instructions.

How could we ever hope to negotiate some 20,000 nautical miles of
flight through and over inhospitable terrain and countries if we could
not understand the first controller we encountered? How would we ever
explain to our friends and sponsors that we could not even depart the

initial airport of the race? We were frustrated and upset. Obviously, the other airplanes would be able to understand, but we were clueless. We taxied back to the ramp and shut down the engine.

Fortunately, one of the race organization personnel was in the tower. Patrick Seurat to the rescue. Patrick came down from the tower and out to our airplane in the pouring rain and explained that the controllers used the three-letter identifiers for VORs when giving instructions. He explained that "Oscar Lima" was OL, the identifier for the Orly VOR. He pointed out that should a French controller say the name of a VOR, for instance the Coulommiers VOR, most English-speaking pilots would have no idea what he said. By using the identifiers, it became understandable to all participants.

The words were barely out of his mouth when we knew exactly what he was talking about. The instructions were clear and made a lot of sense. If we had not been so stressed and anxious about beginning the air race, we would have easily known, as it simply used the alphabetic symbols for the VOR instead of the actual name as we did in the US. We and the controllers at home were accustomed to using the name—the Friant VOR, for example—instead of the alphabetic identifier—FRA or Foxtrot Romeo Alpha.

It would not be so difficult after all. A piece of cake. We could do this. We were quickly given our clearance and were on our way. We felt such a relief when we finally lifted off the ground.

Another difference from flying in the US was that the controller asked for an estimated time of arrival at various points along the route. It was necessary to report passing this point and give our estimated time of arrival at the next one, two, or three points, and also our flight level passing. This information was requested constantly, so a lot of time was spent talking to controllers and performing the computations. We had no calculators, so we had to trust our math skills—sometimes when we were so tired that we could hardly add one plus one. Fortunately, we managed.

Jim and I had decided to alternate flying duties with navigating and communicating, though this was rather loose, depending on the various situations. We departed Paris IFR, and Jim flew the first leg to Kerkira on the island of Corfu, where we were going to refuel. I spoke with the

The panel of our airplane, the *Winged Quest*.

controllers and calculated the times of arrival at the various reporting points and gave them our altitude.

Almost as soon as we broke ground, we entered the clouds. We quickly exited the Paris area, climbed to flight level 190 and were on our way. Icing was no problem, because it was too cold for ice to form. However, it was solid IFR, and we could not see the countryside.

As we climbed through the clouds, I nodded off to sleep for a short power nap. After a restless night with little sleep, I wanted to be certain that I would be awake and alert to take over flying duties for the next leg after Kerkira. Allen was asleep in the seat behind me.

I awoke as we were breaking through the clouds in Italy—just in time to catch a fantastic glimpse of the Alps. Also, it was time to give another position report to the controller. We were flying at 19,000 feet, and the snowcapped mountains and valleys below were breathtaking. We could see Mont Blanc in the distance, though it was not designated on the charts. From then on, neither Jim nor I slept again until we reached Abu Dhabi, United Arab Emirates, the next afternoon.

Approach to the runway at Kerkira, on the island of Corfu.

We were rerouted by the air traffic controller on one occasion, but eventually exited Italy at Brindisi and crossed the first of many nautical miles of overwater flight to enter Greek air space. The total flight from Paris to Corfu took about five and one-half hours. The distance flown was approximately 1,060 nautical miles. Since we had to fly so high, we were using oxygen virtually the entire time from Paris to Corfu. This was to cause some difficulties on our next leg.

We were the first race aircraft to land in Kerkira and were excited to see the customs people and fuel truck come to our airplane immediately. However, the fuel truck refused to fuel us.

The Chronopost team had called from the air, advising them that they had priority, and the truck fueled them first on landing—much to our disgust. The Chronopost team took off while Jim and I were still waiting for the fuel and paperwork. Frustrating!

We learned that Chronopost had a friend on the ground at the airport who arranged this for them. The friend came out to greet them, but they had already left, so he asked Jim and me to convey his best wishes to them. For a time thereafter, we referred to this team as the "compost" team.

In short order, we were refueled, filed a flight plan to Luxor, Egypt, our next planned fuel stop, got a weather briefing, and ate the lunch that had been given to us by the race organization in Toussus-le-Noble—another development, which we would later regret.

We had arrived in Corfu (Kerkira) at about 15:30 local time, since we lost an hour going eastbound, and departed Corfu at about 16:30 local time en route, across the Mediterranean Sea, to Luxor, Egypt.[2] The Greek islands were lush, green, and beautiful, and soon were left behind as the airplane proceeded over its first extensive overwater flight. [Note: I use 24-hour time when in flight and navigation. Otherwise, times are denoted in local 12-hour time.]

Fortunately, the weather was good and the airplane engine purred smoothly as night fell. We could not tell whether we were over land or sea because of the darkness. However, from our charts, we knew that we were over the Mediterranean Sea. Allen soon was asleep. We sailed on through the night at 9,000 feet, no longer having oxygen, as none was available in Kerkira. Not being able to replenish our oxygen was another glitch we had not anticipated. Since we would need oxygen in order to fly at a high altitude, this would be a real problem.

Our Cessna was unpressurized, which meant that we needed supplemental oxygen tanks and oxygen masks not only for Jim and me, but also for Allen. Oxygen was needed any time that we flew above 10,000 feet, and it was more important at night than during the daytime because one's vision is more sensitive to diminished oxygen. It is recommended, though not a rule, that oxygen be used above 6,000 feet at night. The oxygen tanks are located in the ceiling above the pilots and are filled from the outside. The masks hang down from the ceiling, though they can be put away when not needed.

I was flying this leg, which should have been from Kerkira to Luxor. However, since we were unable to obtain oxygen at Kerkira, we had to remain low and could not take the most direct route. Our mandatory position report at Kanar was relayed to Cairo Radio by a helpful airliner. Shortly before arriving at El Daba on the Egyptian coast, Cairo Radio

---

2. We filed R-19 to Didimon (DDM), B-1 to Paleohore (PLH), A-1 to KANAR, W-727 to El Daba (DBA), LUBUS, SENEU, then A-10 to Luxor (LXR).

amended our flight plan to require us to proceed from El Daba along B12 to New Valley (NWV), then W726 to Luxor.

Unfortunately, this route would have added almost 200 additional nautical miles to the flight to Luxor. As filed, the trip would have been about 953 nautical miles and would have taken about five and one-half hours.

The route as proposed by Cairo would have been over 1,150 nautical miles and would have taken over six and one-half hours. The airplane had an optimum range, with reserves of six hours and about 1,050 nautical miles. The reason given by Cairo for requiring the change in the route was that the published en route chart requires an aircraft to fly at flight level 280. We could only fly at flight level 250, even if we had oxygen, which we did not have.

We later learned that many of the other participants simply gave false position reports to make Cairo Radio believe that they were proceeding via New Valley, and then they proceeded virtually direct to Luxor contrary to the controller's instructions and the published limitation on the en route chart. Evidently, as professional pilots, they were aware that there was no radar, so they got away with it.

We did not know that was an option, and since we did not consider violating the rules, our choice was clear, though we were not happy about it. Obviously, we had to stop at Cairo for fuel. We announced our intentions to the controller, who immediately cleared us to Cairo International Airport from El Daba via W727 to Fayoum (FYM), then R-778 to Cairo. Because of smog, we were vectored to Rwy 05R at Cairo International Airport. The lights of Cairo were beautiful as we descended on the approach.

After landing, we had a difficult time following the taxiways and the ground controller's instructions, but eventually we found the so-called isolated parking area. It truly was isolated. We wanted to park close to the terminal, as we simply needed to refuel, file a new flight plan, and leave, and we were both frustrated that this request had been denied, and we were assigned to this dark area so far from the tower. The stop in Cairo was slow, expensive, bureaucratic, and inefficient.

Other commercial aircraft were being refueled, and finally our small airplane was also refueled. Afterward, we had to accompany one of the airport personnel to the terminal to pay the landing fees and complete the numerous forms required. We paid landing fees, taxes, and handling fees of over $285 plus the fuel. It appears that we were charged for more fuel than we actually received, since the fuel consumption between Cairo and Luxor was incredible, and headwinds could not account for all of it.

Then it was necessary to file a flight plan, which necessitated climbing, either by stairs or by an elevator, to the third floor of the tower. We took the elevator after leaving our passports with one of many guards who were prowling around the facility at the entrance to the hallway from which the elevators were located. We were hesitant to do this, as we did not know who he was, his position, or whether we would ever see our passports again, but we were not given a choice.

With the airport representative, we stepped into a smelly elevator. By now, it was about 11:00 at night local time. The elevator operator was dressed in a long, sweaty, and filthy A-line shirt. On closer examination, Jim realized that the shape on the floor of the elevator was a person, similarly dressed, asleep.

We finally filed our flight plan, retrieved our passports, were taken back to our airplane in the isolated parking area, and departed Cairo for Riyadh, which we hoped would be our next fuel stop.

Sunday, March 1, 1987

It was Jim's turn to fly, and after leaving Cairo, it was necessary to fly south to Luxor in order to enter Saudi air space. For some reason, one cannot fly directly from Cairo to Riyadh, but can fly from Luxor to Riyadh. We did the necessary calculations and knew that we could only make Riyadh without refueling again if the winds were favorable, since it was approximately 1,051 nautical miles. No such luck.

Strong headwinds confronted us immediately upon departing from Cairo, and our fuel consumption was astronomical. We had intended to make a left turn at Luxor and fly on to Riyadh, but by the time we arrived in Luxor, we had no choice. The only safe way to fly was to stop again in Luxor, 272 nautical miles south of Cairo, for fuel. We were disappointed that we had to make that extra stop.

We called Luxor tower when we were about 25 miles north of the city and were cleared to land on runway 20. We taxied to the fuel truck, got out, and asked for fuel, which we obtained without delay. Our sponsors had given us items to distribute as gifts, such as raisins, raisin hats, almonds, T-shirts, and posters, and we gave the line crew raisin hats and raisins, which tended to infuriate El Jefe (as we referred to him), who appeared to have some degree of responsibility for assuring that foreign troops were not landing to seize the place. He had the usual array of stars and bars on his shoulders.

Another race airplane landed shortly after us. It was *Bio-France Elevage*, piloted by Gilles Rousseau and François Dabin. After a few minutes, Gilles, Jim, and I were ushered into what appeared to be an empty passenger terminal. El Jefe knocked on a door and, without waiting, barged in on a sleeping Jefe II, who was not amused. He obviously did not like being disturbed in the middle of the night, and certainly not by invaders from France and the United States.

After paying a modest $50 landing fee for each aircraft, we were summarily dismissed by El Jefe II, who would not, on request, stamp our passports. At that point, I went back to the airplane to wait.

Gilles and Jim followed El Jefe to another office, only to again find someone sleeping on the floor. Jim realized that someone was asleep in every office and cubbyhole in the place. When was the next airliner scheduled to land? We were not quite sure, but probably hours from the time of our visit. Apparently, the airport is fully staffed all night, even though no aircraft were scheduled to land.

El Jefe then took Jim and Gilles to the tower to file their flight plans. The tower was located in an old building, which was obviously the old terminal building. It was spooky to walk through the partially lighted facility. Guards were walking or standing about with their submachine guns. Who knows who was sleeping in the shadows.

After walking through the building for some distance, Jim and Gilles climbed the stairs to the tower. Everything was dirty, smelly, and in a state of disrepair. For part of the way, the stairway was not protected by a railing. Any inadvertent misstep would have resulted in a header to the distant filthy floor below.

After making it to the top, they found a fellow perched in front of radios that were out-of-date in 1945. The wind direction and velocity equipment were old, cracked, and practically unusable. El Jefe waited while Jim and Gilles discussed their flight plans with the tower operator. There was only one person working. He soon let it be known that something should be paid to him for his efforts. Jim told him that he did not have any money with him. That was not an accurate statement, but Jim had only $100 bills ($2,000 worth) with him and was not going to share that.

Finally, Jim told him that he would give him $20 but that he had to go to the airplane to get the money from me. The operator said, "No problem, this fellow will go." Whereupon, out of a chair came a young man who had been asleep, wrapped in a blanket or cover of some sort. The boy followed Jim and El Jefe down the rickety stairs to receive payment.

El Jefe then let Jim in on two big secrets. First, he had a masterful command of one English word, *boss*, and second, he also wanted some money. On arriving at the airplane, Jim gave the boy, El Jefe, and two other hangers-on $20 each, and we started the engine and left. We felt bad for all the people we saw there who seemed to be so poor and needy.

We had spent the whole night in Egyptian airports, and by the time we left Luxor, it was 05:00 local time. We filed the same flight plan as we had filed in Cairo—from Luxor to Riyadh.

By the time we reached the Red Sea, the sun's first rays peeked over the horizon and extended like long fingers that blended together as they reached toward the sky. As they bent forward, they gently touched the earth, illuminating the Red Sea and eastern coast of Saudi Arabia. It was beautiful.

The sand in the desert had been blown into swirling patterns and reached right to the bank of the sea. The sun became a red ball, probably colored by the sand and dust in the air. We were exhausted after being awake for twenty-four hours, but we had a feeling of wonder and excitement, not only because of the panorama, which had just appeared ahead, but also by the thought of just being there. We thought of the long history of this area we were about to enter.

It would have been my turn to fly this leg from Luxor to Riyadh and Jim's turn to communicate with the controllers, but we had decided that since women cannot drive in Saudi Arabia, it would cause a problem if I flew or spoke to the Saudi controllers, and we didn't want to create any issue that might result in a delay. We agreed that Jim should fly and also speak to air traffic control on the radio.

I was definitely not happy about this restriction and thought back to other times in my life when I had been told that I could not do something because I was a woman. However, I recognized the situational necessity and reluctantly behaved.

At the appointed time, we reached Jeddah control. The first controller was difficult to understand, but after the appropriate number of "Say again please" requests, we mastered the instructions. The second controller spoke English with an American accent. When asked if we could fly at 9,000 feet instead of the minimum flight level of 190 prescribed by the en route chart, he answered, "It's okay with me." This was good news since we had not been able to get oxygen in Cairo or Luxor and had none left.

Allen snapped one picture after another, and I took videos and pictures. Jim dutifully flew the airplane. Shortly thereafter, Jim was speaking to a person at Jeddah control who was nearly impossible to understand. At some point, he stopped speaking to us altogether.

At first, we thought that it was because Jim kept asking him to repeat or "say again," but later we realized that we were simply out of his range at our low altitude. He had not handed us off to another controller, so this resulted in our flying about 400 miles across the majority of Saudi Arabia without speaking to any controller at all.

We encountered a horrible summer storm with wind, rain, a little hail, plus sand. We bounced around and had to fly low, under the storm. It was frustrating that we had not been able to obtain oxygen so that we could have flown above it. Finally, the weather cleared, and it was smooth flying again.

We were now flying quite close to Riyadh air space and still had not spoken to a controller. This was dangerous, as we assumed that if an unidentified airplane flew into Riyadh air space without permission, it may be intercepted or even shot down. This part of the world was volatile. We did not know the appropriate frequency, and there were no other race participants in the vicinity that we could ask.

Jim tried to contact any commercial carrier that might be nearby, but he received no response. We finally agreed that perhaps a female voice might get a response, so I transmitted on the radio in my most sweet, feminine voice and asked whether anyone at all could hear me.

Immediately I received a response from a pilot flying for a Saudi oil company. He relayed our position and expected landing time to Riyadh and gave us the appropriate frequency, and we were cleared to enter their air space.

Again, we experienced high wind, severe turbulence, and heavy rain as we approached Riyadh and had to penetrate some black clouds. It appeared to be the fringe of a thunderstorm, and we hoped that it would clear up before we had to land. The stormscope showed where the bad cells were located, and we were able to avoid the worst of them. Finally, the weather cleared and at about 10:00 local time, we landed at Riyadh.

The Saudi oil company pilot who had relayed our position also landed at Riyadh and came over to our airplane to meet us. He said that he was surprised to hear my voice on the radio and wondered what a woman was doing flying in Saudi Arabia. I said "Well, women *do* fly." He answered, "Yes, in the rest of the world, but not here."

The King Khalid International Airport in Riyadh is beautiful and one of the most modern airports in the world. The main terminal is striking architecturally and almost organic. We were across the field at the general aviation terminal, which also was one of the largest and most modern that we had seen. It was impressive. The personnel were helpful and interested in our airplane. A couple of US pilots also were there, flying for Saudi companies, and they seemed happy to meet other pilots from home.

After refueling, obtaining some light refreshments from a vending machine, and a weather briefing, we filed a new flight plan from Riyadh to Abu Dhabi.

When we started the airplane to leave for Abu Dhabi, our radios did not work at all. "Now what!" we wondered. We played around with them for a while, checked the circuit breakers and other items. Then a man came to our airplane and told us to move about 20 feet, as there were some dead spots on the tarmac where radios would not transmit. As soon as we moved, our radios worked perfectly. We were relieved, taxied, and took off.

Our approach to the runway to land in Abu Dhabi.

From Riyadh, we had to fly northeast over Bahrain and out into the Persian Gulf to the Motta intersection before heading down the gulf to Abu Dhabi.[3] One cannot fly directly from Riyadh to Abu Dhabi over Qatar, or the airplane would be intercepted. We had been given instructions at the initial briefing in Paris regarding what we should do if we were intercepted, but we were not sure that we would remember them if the need actually arose and certainly hoped that it never would.

The Motta intersection is approximately the area where the American frigate USS *Stark* was hit two months later by Iraqi shells. We could see the Iranian coast on our left, Qatar on our right, and various oil tankers and other ships in the gulf below. We also flew over many oil rigs in the gulf, some of which were blown up a couple of months later.

On this day, however, everything seemed peaceful, and we headed down the gulf without incident. The weather was still marginal until we were approaching Abu Dhabi, when it cleared. We arrived there at

---

3. The route was G-53 to KARAB, then Dhahran (DHA) and Bahrain (BAH) A-1 to Motta, then G-462 to Abu Dhabi (AUH).

approximately 4:30 p.m.—about thirty-two hours after leaving Paris—dead tired and starving.

In Paris, we had each been given a substantial lunch to take with us on the airplane, but inasmuch as we landed in Corfu about noon, we ate our lunch and threw away the excess food. Not a good decision, as there was nothing to eat in either Cairo or Luxor. We found no food at all until Riyadh, where we had a small cheese sandwich. That night in Abu Dhabi, we had a nice dinner and ate every bite. Then we went to bed early, as we were exhausted.

4

Abu Dhabi

Monday, March 2, 1987

The United Arab Emirates, and Abu Dhabi in particular, is one of the wealthiest places on earth, judged on a per capita income basis. The city of Abu Dhabi, situated on the southeastern shore of the Persian Gulf, is modern. It is the capital of the United Arab Emirates, which is a collection of seven small sheikhdoms, or emirates, which had been established about fifteen years earlier.

The tremendous prosperity arising from oil production transformed this once small, sleepy village into a modern city of perhaps 100,000 persons when we were there. It has grown substantially since then. Many high-rise buildings punctuated the skyline, including the ten-story Holiday Inn, which was our home for the two nights that we were there.

The sheikhs have built huge palaces with every modern amenity along the man-made waterways that crisscross the place. Actually, these abodes were not palaces as we would picture them, but instead are massive compounds that include several large homes that house the extended family.

The Persian Gulf was a troubled place. The Iran-Iraq war had been under way for years at the gulf's north end. The Iranians had threatened to stop the passage of tankers through the Strait of Hormuz, through which

New mosque in Abu Dhabi.

they must pass to take on the liquid gold—petroleum—at the various oil ports in Kuwait, Saudi Arabia, United Arab Emirates, and others.

Jim awoke early to the sound of the call to prayer just outside our window. I was so tired that I don't think a cannon could have awakened me, so I slept through it and woke at a much later hour.

We were still hungry after our Paris to Abu Dhabi flight, so we ate a good and substantial breakfast before going to the airport to refuel and get oxygen. We had obtained some fuel in Riyadh, but we wanted to top off the tanks. In Abu Dhabi, there was oxygen, but no fitting that would work. They use metric fittings, and of course ours were standard or English fittings. This was another of the glitches we had not anticipated.

Our airplane was fueled by state or government workers from fifty-five-gallon barrels. Even though Abu Dhabi is one of the richest oil-producing countries in the world, they do not have 100-octane fuel for private aircraft. The private aircraft that ordinarily stop there are jets or turbine-engine aircraft that require jet fuel, not piston aircraft that require 100-octane fuel.

Jim and I and La Girafe with our airplane in Abu Dhabi.

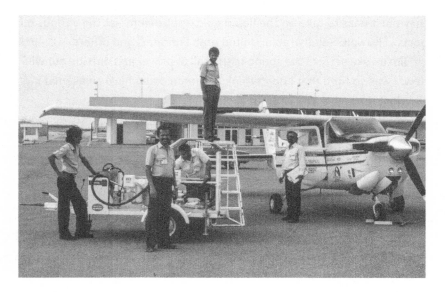

Refueling in Abu Dhabi with more personnel than necessary.

Sufficient fuel had been brought in specially for our general aviation airplanes in tanks that had to be hand-pumped. The government personnel who were refueling the airplanes looked more like the Keystone Cops rather than an efficient fueling operation. It took at least a dozen people to refuel each airplane: one on the ladder, one to hold the hose, one to check the gauges, one to check the pumps, and at least a half dozen others to stand around, watch, and supervise. Of course, I had to take a picture.

The FBO at Abu Dhabi airport, Emirates Air Service, is operated by Eric Bostick, who was formerly from the US. He once commented that he had a colorful and interesting life. He said that he had been in the United Arab Emirates for a number of years. His two chief workers were also from the US (one may have been from Canada) and were nice young men who evidently landed in the UAE because the money was so good.

Eric and the boys let us know early on that they could have refueled us quickly and efficiently but were precluded from doing so because the government wanted to be involved in this operation due to the publicity that the race was receiving.

Eric and his crew were helpful in other ways, however, and tried to get us oxygen. They also washed our windshields. Eric also agreed to ship home some of the luggage that we had brought with us, and we left it with him. We could not wait to rid ourselves of the extra luggage and appreciated his offer.

We returned to the hotel, showered, attended a press conference that was conducted in English, French, and Arabic, and then ate at a beautiful banquet on the roof of the Holiday Inn. Eric and the boys were there and seemed pleased to be around us and talk to people from home.

It was a gorgeous night, the food consisted of all local dishes, which were excellent. We met some people from the American Embassy and expat community, including Donna Clark and her husband, Sam, who sold missiles. We had never met a missile salesman before, but assumed that it was a common occupation in this part of the world.

There was entertainment and belly dancing. The lead dancer was Miss Lebanon. A sheikh, or some type of minister, came with his long, white tobe under a luxurious black robe trimmed with gold. He gave a speech,

A press conference about the air race was held in Abu Dhabi.
Patricia, Bernard Lamy's daughter, (from left); an official from Abu
Dhabi; Bernard Lamy; Gerard Emler; and another local race official.

Allen Funch, on the left, me, and Jim on the right with
students in Abu Dhabi. We are showing them a poster from
the International English Institute, one of our sponsors.

and I gave him presents from our sponsors. He liked the International English Institute T-shirt the best. He told us that he could not wear it, but he was showing it to all of his friends, and we were told that he would wear it in private.

Tuesday, March 3, 1987

We were leaving today, but Donna Clark asked that we stop by her grade school in the morning, and her husband picked us up at the hotel. At the school, we spoke with the children, one of whom was the grandchild of the head sheikh. They loved the gifts of raisins and T-shirts from our sponsors and were particularly interested in the International English Institute, one of our sponsors, which was a language school that taught English to students from around the world.

We also stopped by the American Embassy, which was not guarded or at all secure. There had never been any problems so far, but we were told that they intended to install some security soon, as things were not stable in the region. We were surprised that there was not more security already.

5

Abu Dhabi to Dhaka

Tuesday, March 3, 1987

Winged Quest reestablished herself as a flying machine at 10:40, sailing forth into perhaps the best weather of the entire race. The sky was blue, clear, and fresh with even a slight tailwind to add to our optimism that we would have a great flight on this leg of our journey.

The airplane seemed to feel happy as it purred along comfortably, and we were also. It was magic, and our spirits were high. The flight from Abu Dhabi to Dhaka would be much shorter than our previous leg, and we hoped that we might even arrive in time for a late dinner.

I flew the first leg, Abu Dhabi to Muscat, over the Persian Gulf, past Iran, to the Jiwani intersection, and past Afghanistan to Ahmedabad, India.[4] Perhaps showing some concern for a potential conflict with the Iranians, the Pakistanis had turned us to the right before we reached the Jiwani VOR (JI), which is only about 14 nautical miles from Iran. We thought about the hostage crisis that had occurred several years earlier and decided that we definitely would avoid any contact with Iran. It even felt eerie to be so close.

---

4. Our IFR flight plan called for B-55 to Seeb (MCT), R-462 to DENDA, then, thanks to the Pakistani controllers, a 90-degree right turn direct to LATEM, A-1S to TALEM, G-472ED to SOGAR and VASLA, then G-472E to Ahmedabad, India.

Chuck Rosenquist, the American pilot of the *Vail Snail*, evidently did not feel as we did, as he called a controller in Iran when he approached the Iranian coast. After a conversation of several minutes, the controller suddenly asked, "By the way, what nationality are you?" Whereupon the Piper Malibu had a sudden, irremediable radio failure that was not fixed until the next radio communication with a Pakistani controller.

The overwater portion of this flight was over 500 nautical miles and involved estimating fixes by reference to our watch and a compass. It is a rather helpless feeling to look around and see nothing but water in every direction. Our overwater position reports were relayed by airliners and other race aircraft in contact with Pakistani and eventually Indian controllers.

Our navigation was flawless, and we arrived over the coast of India after the overwater portion at exactly the right location and within five minutes of the estimated time of arrival. We agreed that this was a great day and a beautiful flight.

We made good time and arrived in Ahmedabad, India, ahead of schedule, at about 16:15 local time. A large crowd had gathered to catch a view of our aircraft. Chronopost was leaving as we arrived.

We were shown into an old building without windows (they were all broken out), which had served as an early terminal for the airport. What was unusual is that it appeared that there also was a second, abandoned terminal building on the airfield.

In the building, several old tables and chairs represented each station for the incoming aircraft. One station was for paying for fuel, the other for the payment of landing fees, one for immigration, and others that were unknown to anyone outside of India. The local aero club apparently had arranged the whole thing, and they efficiently processed each crew. We were impressed.

The bathrooms were quite an adventure on this trip. In Ahmedabad, when I asked a guard for the *toilette*, he seemed embarrassed and pointed toward a wooden fence, perhaps five feet high and five feet across, in back and to the right of the "terminal" building. I walked down the path toward the fence, and behind it I found a small U-shaped room with no door. This contained only a urinal, and since it was open on one

I talked with townspeople and children who were allowed out
of school to greet the airplanes in Ahmedabad, India.

side and not completely screened from the tarmac by the fence, I was
not inclined to use it.

To the right and adjoining was another U-shaped cubicle, and this one
had a door of sorts on the appropriate side. I walked in, expecting to see
a toilet, or even a urinal. There was none. There was simply a hole in the
ground, albeit ceramic, with a ceramic foot-stand on each side. There was
also a waterspout and bucket, obviously to "flush" the debris down the
ceramic hole.

This was quite manageable, and I was in no danger of locking myself
in, as there was no lock on the door. As I left the room to return to the
tarmac, one of the guards was utilizing the urinal next to me. He was quite
friendly and seemed pleased to meet me and greeted me as I walked by. I
remained cool and gave him a friendly nod, but it was a strange sensation
to be greeted by a stranger who was urinating.

I asked the security people if I could talk with the townspeople who
had gathered behind the fence. At first my request was denied, and I was
also told that we could take no pictures. Soon, however, the head security

officer came over to me and said that I could go to the fence if I did not bring any of the locals onto the field. Also, I could take some pictures.

This was a big event in Ahmedabad, and they had even cancelled school so that their children could come out to see these airplanes from various countries that were stopping in their city. The people asked questions and were extremely friendly. Of course I brought La Girafe, who was quite a hit. Everyone wanted to touch me—not in a hostile way, but just a gentle touch. Perhaps they wanted to see if I was real.

We would have been in and out in twenty minutes, except that just as the fuel truck pulled up to our airplane, the fuel pump broke, and it took two hours to fix it. They were so embarrassed, and we felt badly for them because they had tried so hard to have everything perfect for us. They wanted to pour the fuel through a dirty funnel, but Jim would not permit it. After a delay, they succeeded in fixing the truck, and the refueling proceeded without incident. They gave us gifts of a cloth binder and sandwiches.

We finally got back into the air at sundown or 18:05 local time. The next leg of our flight was primarily at night, so we did not see much of India, which was disappointing. We had hoped to see much more of the countryside.[5]

East of Nagpur, the team from Hong Kong, David Beechcroft-Kay, Kevin Hoban, and Bonnie Engel in *Spirit of Hong Kong* (which we referred to as Hotel Echo, the last letters of its tail number) experienced a problem. They were at 15,000 feet, and we were at 13,000 feet. We were in contact with Calcutta radio, but they were not, so they asked us to relay their request to descend to a lower altitude, as they had an oxygen leak. Calcutta would not allow them to descend, as they were only about 10 nautical miles behind us, and Calcutta was concerned about the separation.

We offered to descend lower, and they agreed that we could descend to 11,000 feet, and they brought Hotel Echo down to 13,000 feet. Unfortunately, Hotel Echo had completely run out of oxygen. They pleaded with the controller to give them a lower flight level, but nothing would move the controller, who insisted that they must remain at 13,000 feet.

5. The route to Dhaka was G-472 to BODAR, DAKOS, Nagpur (NNP,) G-450 to Calcutta (CEA) then A-462 to Dhaka, Bangladesh.

We surmised that it must be, at least in part, prompted by the fact that we were flying just ahead and practically beneath *Spirit of Hong Kong*. This was still too high for them at night without oxygen, so we advised Calcutta control that we would descend to 9,000 feet so they could bring Hotel Echo lower; however, control refused.

We knew that this was dangerous for them, so we made our own arrangements with Hotel Echo to come down to our level, with us flying to the left of the airway and them to the right. They could see our lights, and we could safely maintain our own separation. We did not report our positions (or their altitude) to control, of course. We had learned from our experience in Egypt that it was sometimes necessary to be slightly deceptive.

Soon, we were able to contact Dhaka control, and we all were able to descend to a safe level and land. The Hong Kong crew was very appreciative, and we later became good friends.

The distance between Ahmedabad and Dhaka is about 1,042 nautical miles. After six hours and at 02:00 local time, we landed in Dhaka. We were met by personnel from the organization as always, plus the airport manager and other miscellaneous military types. As usual, all of the guards were armed to the teeth. We were shown into the VIP lounge and processed by immigration, and I immediately fell asleep on a couch. It seemed as though I was always falling asleep in chairs, on couches, or wherever we were. Shortly after, we were taken to the hotel for food and some much-needed rest.

6

Dhaka, Bangladesh

Wednesday, March 4, 1987

Dhaka is the capital and one of the oldest cities of Bangladesh. It began as an urbanized settlement dating from the seventh century and was ruled by many kingdoms or dynasties, including the Mughals, before coming under British rule for 150 years until the independence of India. It then became the capital of the East Bengal province under the Dominion of Pakistan.

After the independence of Bangladesh in 1971, Dhaka became the capital of the new state. In 1982, the English spelling of the city was officially changed from Dacca to Dhaka. After independence, political turmoil continued and was heightened in the mid-1980s with a pro-democracy movement. Political and student strikes and protests were routine. However, the period also has seen massive growth and a real estate boom.

When we were there, we found the people to be friendly and full of hope. We often heard: "We are still a young country, but we are going to succeed."

Our hotel in Dhaka, the Sonargaon, was one of the nicest on the trip. We fell into bed about 4:00 a.m. and were then supposed to go to the airport to refuel at 9:00 a.m. I slept in and Jim went. I was sleeping so soundly that I was only vaguely aware when he left.

Later, I took La Girafe to breakfast and then relaxed by the pool
and swam. Jim was at the airport
until 4:00 p.m., as the fuel, again,
had to be hand-pumped from
barrels. He did not eat all day,
and since he had eaten little the
day before while we were flying,
he did not feel well. No sleep, no
food, just exhaustion.

The National Sports Control
Board planned a reception for us
in the afternoon, and we all were
encouraged to attend. A couple
of buses drove us through the
city to the Sports Board building, which was warm and stuffy
inside. The carpeting was an old
green shag, and the walls were
wood paneled. There were no

In Dhaka, Bangladesh,
with contrasts between low
shacks and tall buildings.

windows, and bench-type seating in a large circle faced the podium. At
one side of the room was an array of finger food.

After a long wait, the speeches began. Some were not in English, and
we were handed a written translation to read along with the speaker. After
the speeches, we moved toward the food tables, but the electricity went
out, and it was totally dark. We waited a few minutes and then left. We had
felt obligated to listen to the long speeches but were happy to finally be
out of there.

A large crowd had gathered as we returned to the bus, and we could
hardly move through them. At one point I thought that I would be sepa-
rated and carried away by the crowd, but some of the other competitors
came to my rescue and cleared the way for me. I did not feel threatened,
but rather that I might be crushed by the curious crowd of onlookers,
who kept pushing in against me, wanting to touch me.

In the evening, a banquet was held around the swimming pool at the hotel, with many important ministers—everyone who was anyone in Bangladesh officialdom. Jim stayed for about five minutes and then went to our room for some much-needed sleep. I stayed and was nearly finished with dinner when it was announced that a monsoon-type storm was expected with 50-mile-per-hour winds, rain, and hail.

Fortunately, I was seated at the table with the Hotel Echo pilots, David Beechcroft-Kay and Kevin Hoban, and the British High Commissioner. I was invited to join them, and we left immediately for the airport in the High Commissioner's Rolls-Royce with British flags flying. David obtained permission from Biman, the Bangladesh airline, to put our two airplanes inside their hangar.

We rushed out to our airplanes. The airport manager was there, and we told him what we were intending to do, and that some people from Biman were coming to assist. He was okay with that, but somewhat concerned because, of course, this was not part of his instructions. He had simply been instructed to guard the airplanes or take care of them.

The Biman people arrived, and one of the engineers boarded David's airplane. I was told to follow them to the Biman hangar in my airplane. The winds already were strong, and it was raining. We were obtaining taxi clearance from the tower when the pilots of some of the other airplanes, who had taken taxis to the airport, began arriving and coming onto the tarmac.

The airport manager became concerned and motioned for me to cut my engine. I would not, because I knew that if I did, he would never allow me to start it again, and I would not be able to taxi to safety. One of his people came over and banged on the window of my airplane, motioning for me to cut my engine. I shook my head no and got back on the radio with David and the tower for taxi instructions.

Two guys from the organization's technical team came over to the airplane, and I opened the window. They told me to shut down the engine because the airport manager was getting upset, and they thought that I was going to cause problems with the airport people. I told them that I had permission to taxi, I was going to the Biman hangar, that I had permission to put our airplane in there, and that no bureaucrat was going to keep me on the tarmac unless he was prepared to pay for any damages to our $200,000-plus airplane—and I wanted the money in advance!

They backed off, and I began to taxi, along with the Hotel Echo 335, but after about 100 yards down the taxiway, the tower instructed us both to hold. The airport manager had contacted them on his handheld radio and told the tower that we were not to leave the area. David had to get the Biman engineer on the radio to talk to the tower, and after much argument, we finally were both allowed to taxi to the Biman hangar.

We could not get our airplanes into the hangar because there was a large airliner in it. Therefore, we stopped the airplanes outside, one to the right and the other to the left of the airliner, and they moved the airliner out. We then pushed the 335 and our Cessna 210 inside. This was all done in wind and rain, which kept increasing until both airplanes were in.

We all breathed a sigh of relief. Then the winds died down.

We returned to the hotel after midnight and had a soda (no liquor served after 11:00 p.m.). The fellow from the organization who had instructed me to comply with the airport manager's demands arrived and began scolding me for not complying.

I looked at him as though he must be crazy, and David absolutely took him on and told him that I was the captain of my aircraft and had a duty to make certain that it was safe. Neither he nor the aircraft manager could do that, so I had acted properly. He was at least partially apologetic.

I finally got into bed about 1:00 a.m. David was my protector that evening, and I was happy that we had facilitated him flying at a safe altitude the night before.

Thursday, March 5, 1987

The next morning, it was Jim's turn to relax, so Kevin, one of the Hotel Echo pilots, and I decided to go to the airport at 9:00 a.m. to try to get oxygen for our airplanes. A driver from Biman picked us up, but on the way to the airport, we nearly ended up in the middle of a riot.

We were driving across a railroad track, approaching an intersection, when we saw hundreds of people running toward the intersection from our left, waving sticks and shouting. Immediately to our right stood uniformed officers with helmets, shields, clubs, and guns. This was one of the riots we had heard about, and we were about to drive into the middle of it, just as the forces were converging.

Fortunately, there was an alley parallel to the tracks, and our driver was quick. He did a sharp 90-degree turn and headed down the alley. We bumped through huge mud holes, at about 90 miles per hour, dodging cows, people, babies, and rickshaws. This went on for several miles, but the driver was absolutely great. He managed to steer through the obstacles at a high rate of speed while bouncing in and out of the mud holes and sliding sideways in the mud.

We had no seat belts, but managed to hang on. It was one of the best examples of driving skill that I had seen in a long time. Unfortunately, I did not bring my camera. We finally reached the rear of the rioters and headed on toward the airport.

The people at Biman and Haeco, the maintenance organization, were extremely helpful. Biman is an agent for Cathay Pacific, and since David was a Cathay Pacific captain, he and Kevin were able to arrange for their help. Since we were David's friends, they attended to our airplane as well.

There were some problems in obtaining the oxygen, as it was not ordinarily available. No general aviation aircraft requiring oxygen landed here, so, initially, the personnel had to find oxygen. A tank containing approximately 2,000 pounds was available, but it was across town. After it was located, they had to determine whether we could have it or buy it, who would transport it, when, from where, and how much it would cost. This took a good portion of the morning, but finally there was a tank of oxygen available at the hangar.

The next problem was how to get the oxygen from the tank into our airplane. Again, their hookup was metric and we were not, so a fitting had to be made. This was done, and Haeco personnel began replenishing Kevin's oxygen supply. They gave him 1,200 pounds and were ready to begin resupplying our airplane, but it was chow time.

The crew went to lunch, but first they took Kevin and me to the main terminal so that we could eat as well. We all returned about 2:00 p.m., and after more discussion, they put 1,000 pounds of oxygen in our airplane. One of their gauges did not work correctly, so I could not obtain more.

After that, there was about an hour's discussion regarding obtaining small, individual oxygen tanks. These evidently are used on the airlines, and they obtained four small tanks—two for me and two for Kevin—but these small canisters fit the airline masks, not ours. Kevin had some airline masks from Cathay Pacific that he could use, but I had none. One of the Haeco workers solved the problem, however, and lifted a proper mask for me from an airliner.

The people were so nice and helpful and were not going to charge us anything for keeping our airplanes in their hangar for the night or working all day to obtain oxygen for us. Kevin and I decided to give them something, so we each put $150 in an envelope, closed it, and gave it to the head person, telling him to distribute it among the workers. He seemed distracted, put the envelope into his pocket, and walked away.

Approximately fifteen minutes later, he came back with the envelope, which he had opened. He told us that he and his workers did not want to accept any money, and he wished to return it all to us.

We protested and told him that we would be happy to give them the money as a gift for all of their assistance, but he was also insistent and told us that they were honored that the air race had chosen their city for a mandatory stopover, and that they were honored to help us and work on our airplanes. They simply would not take any compensation or gift of any type. In a country as poor as Bangladesh, $300 must have meant a great deal. These people were special.

We returned to the hotel about 5:00 p.m. after obtaining about half of the oxygen we needed. We had missed the rickshaw tour and group photo, but Jim and I hired a driver to drive us around the city to see the sights.

Just before we left for the city tour, Jim and I were in the lobby of the Hotel Sonargaon, talking with David and Kevin, the Cathay Pacific pilots, and looking at the schedule of events. They were complaining about their landing in Corfu and said that one of the Italian teams had cut ahead of them in the pattern, forcing them to veer off to avoid a collision. They were quite angry and confronted the Italians and had a few words after landing.

We told them about our experience with the Chronopost team refueling ahead of us in Corfu. Just then a rather distinguished-looking gentleman who was standing nearby said, "Excuse me, I am the father of one of the Chronopost team members. Is there a problem?"

He was extremely upset that we were critical of his team and that the members had misbehaved, since he was sponsoring the airplane in this race to publicize his postal service. It is similar to our FedEx, and he wanted to establish goodwill. We toned down our explanation somewhat, and he assured us that there would be no more problems.

That night we attended a reception at the French ambassador's residence. We had a buffet dinner with local food, well prepared, and very good. "Papa Chronopost" (we did not know his first name, so we thought that would be an appropriate nickname for him) was there and asked us which of the Chronopost members had refused to speak to us at the first dinner.

I assured him that it was not his son or Patrick, who was quite nice. We were hesitant to accuse anyone, but subsequently all of the Chronopost team began speaking to us, on occasion. The next morning, I saw the one who had been shy at the initial dinner in the hall of the hotel, and he went out of his way to say hello. This absolutely floored me, as it was the first time that he had spoken.

Papa Chronopost and his wife, who joined us in Beijing and met us in Paris, both went out of their way to be friendly. Chronopost was opening up markets in various countries and began deliveries in one country while we were there. Therefore, PR was quite important to them.

Because of the flight level problems, the adventure of getting our airplanes in the Biman hangar, and the day of working together to get oxygen, the Cathay Pacific team, David and Kevin, became great friends of ours. Actually, they were good enough friends to request a loan of $600 in US dollars to purchase fuel, which they assured us would be repaid immediately when we reached their home base of Hong Kong. And, of course, we loaned them the money.

7

Dhaka to Kunming

Friday, March 6, 1987

The day that we were to leave Dhaka, many townspeople came to the airport to watch us from a balcony overlooking the tarmac. The Haeco and Biman people, as well as the security personnel, were all there to say goodbye and see us off.

I began taking Polaroid pictures of some of the workers, and suddenly I was quite popular. Even the security men who were more aloof yet curious began coming over and requesting pictures. The chief of security was particularly aloof, but after a short while, one of his assistants came over and told me that the chief would really appreciate having his picture taken. I did so, and he was quite pleased.

Shortly afterward, I went into the terminal building and saw the chief coming out. He already had gone into a little shop and bought a special frame for his picture, which he showed to me, all smiles. La Girafe also was popular and appeared in many of the photos.

The driver from Biman who had driven us down that back alley the day of the riot was there, but unfortunately, my Polaroid film ran out as I was going to take his picture. We nearly were ready to leave, so I did not have time to change film, although I could tell that he was quite disappointed. I took his picture with my 35mm camera and promised to send him a copy.

Airport workers posing with our airplane in Dhaka.

On the morning of March 6, 1987, at 9:20 local time, we departed Dhaka for Kunming, China, our point of entry into mysterious Cathay. I flew and Jim was seated in the right seat, navigating. The weather was beautiful. There were only a few scattered clouds, which added some fluffy white to the blue sky and green countryside.

As we left Bangladesh, the landscape looked much like the middle of the United States. There were plots of land being farmed, houses, roads, rivers, and what appeared to be a rich agricultural area. After a while the terrain began to change, with low foothills gradually becoming higher and more rugged. We flew over the Ganges, muddy and wide, and looked off in the distance, trying to see the higher peaks of the Himalayas through the gathering clouds.[6]

At our briefing, held the afternoon before our departure, Bernard Lamy warned us about flying across Burma (now Myanmar) on any route

---

6. Our IFR (we always filed IFR) flight plan called for a 09:20 (3:20Z) departure. The route was G-463 to Chittagong (CTG), then A-599 to CHILA, A-99 to Lashio (LS), then LINSO, located on the Burma/China border, and then A-599 to Kunming (KMG).

other than A-99 to Lashio from Chittagong. He said that the Burmese were fighting guerillas in northern Burma and that if we were forced to land in the north, no one would be able to rescue us. The required route took us just north of Mandalay, Burma.

Notwithstanding this admonition by Bernard, some of the crews cut straight across from Dhaka to Lashio (even perhaps to Kunming) rather than flying first to Chittagong. Fortunately, no one had a problem. As usual, we took the more cautious route.

Our flight "over the hump" was thrilling and interesting. We crossed the Himalayas at 15,000 feet. The views were spectacular; however, we were too far east to see Mount Everest and the other high peaks. Small towns nestled in the valleys and on the plateaus, and one could only marvel at the isolation of these towns and their ability to survive in this sparsely populated area.

A few puffy clouds floated below us, sometimes more, sometimes fewer, and sometimes they piled up like whipped cream against the deep blue sky. In some areas there were lakes and rivers, and in other areas, the landscape looked dry and barren. Sometimes the land appeared rich and green, and in other places, sandy beige or brown. Always it was interesting, fascinating, and beautiful.

We were excited to be flying over the Burma Road of World War II fame. Just to say Mandalay, Lashio, or Kunming brought memories of long-ago battles between Japanese and Allied forces, of truck convoys carrying much-needed supplies to the tenacious Chinese, and of brave American pilots in P-40s, colorfully painted to intimidate the enemy, attacking Zeros in defense of the Burma Road and the C-47s (DC-3s) flying the "hump."

Fortunately, on the day that we flew over the hump, nothing larger than an occasional bird threatened our flight.

As we approached Kunming, our excitement heightened. This was the headquarters of the historic Flying Tigers, an American Volunteer Group of the Chinese Air Force in 1941 and 1942 under General Claire Chennault. We were about to land where these heroic pilots had landed.

It was a beautiful, sunny day without clouds. The airfield is situated near a lake, and as we flew over a final ridge, we could see the lake perhaps 20 miles ahead, with the city and the runway beyond. We entered

Landscape over Burma.

the downwind and landed on runway 21. The landing was smooth, and as we turned onto the taxiway, we saw green-uniformed guards stationed along the runway and taxiway with rifles held upright against their bodies, standing at attention to greet us.

As I taxied in, we began excitedly waving to them. At first, they seemed reluctant to wave back, but shortly, they broke into big grins, holding their rifles aloft and waving them enthusiastically.

It truly was a historic day. It was the first time since the revolution that a group of general aviation aircraft had been allowed to land in the People's Republic of China. I was the first American female private pilot to land there (though commercial pilots had) since the revolution when Mao took power in 1949. This landing in Kunming was one of the high points of our trip.

We were directed into a parking spot, and I had to switch off the engine immediately, as we were besieged by television cameras and reporters. Cameras rolled and clicked, and the microphones were activated for the inevitable interviews.

As I opened the airplane door, they crowded toward us, preventing our departure before answering their questions. A young woman official approached and pushed her way through. She asked, "English or French?"

When I responded, "English," she informed us that she was our interpreter and that we had to clear customs before we could respond further to the assembled media.

She guided us toward a small brick building that appeared to be left over from the days of World War II and the Flying Tigers. Three or four people sat in folding chairs in front of the building, and we were told that they would be offering us tea after we processed through customs inside.

I had taken La Girafe from the airplane when we exited, and he was tucked under my arm as Jim and I entered the makeshift customs office, still trailed by the reporters and cameras, to complete the required forms. We sat down, forms were thrust in front of us, and reporters were still trying to question us.

We sat at a long table that was covered with a linen tablecloth, and behind it were approximately ten to twelve officials in full uniform, braids, epaulets, medals, stripes, and all. They looked serious, and I was not certain how they would react to this undignified display, and particularly to me, dressed in my red flight suit with a stuffed giraffe under my arm. I looked down, trying to be serious and respectful and concentrated on completing the forms.

The interpreter came to my side and, indicating the giraffe, said, "Does he have a passport?" I looked up at her, not knowing exactly how to respond appropriately.

She then said, "They [the officials] want to know, does he have a valid visa?"

At that point, I realized that this was not a serious question, and looked over at the officials, who were all smiling at their joke. Shortly, they started laughing and talking among themselves, and a couple of them came over to scratch the giraffe behind its ears and stroke its long neck. Shortly, everyone was laughing and joining in the fun. What a relief!

The forms were not terribly numerous, and some of them were in Chinese. We were simply directed to the signature line and signed as indicated. We paid our fees and were ready to depart in short order.

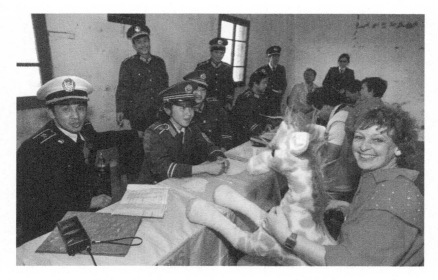

La Girafe and I are clearing customs in Kunming
while the officials laugh at their joke.

After departing from customs, I urgently needed to find a restroom. No private aircraft had landed in Kunming since the revolution, and there is no terminal building, thus no restrooms. I asked the young, English-speaking interpreter as we finished with customs where a *toilette* might be. She pointed toward a corrugated fence, approximately five feet high, between the tarmac and the runway and about 75 yards out across a field.

I headed toward it, through the dry weeds, which sometimes were knee high. I had seen no one else head in that direction, so I was rather surprised when Patrick Grandperret, one of the pilots from the Chronopost team, came from behind the fence. He was just as surprised to see me.

I asked if there were any other occupants on the other side of the fence, and he assured me there were not. I then asked him to wait, guarding my privacy, so that no one else shared my space, and he agreed to do so. It was particularly important on this occasion, since there was not only no private stall, but nothing at all behind the metal corrugated fence except for a hole in the ground, which was meant to be straddled.

My privacy was also important since I had worn a one-piece red flight suit and had to undress almost totally to use the facilities.

With my Chronopost guard in place, there was no interruption, but it did seem strange to not even have the protection of three walls, let alone four. In addition, there was nothing but more knee-high grass between the hole in the ground and the runway, so timing was important. I had to undress between landing and departing flights. Fortunately, the field was large and my timing was good.

Refueling in Kunming with
boy standing on wing.

Jim had seen to the refueling of our airplane, during which one Chinese line boy got on top of the airplane wing and walked about—something that is never done. Jim did not say anything. What could he say anyway? The boy did not speak English and Jim did not speak Chinese. At least we were being refueled.

I returned to the tarmac, and Jim and I sipped tea in front of the brick customs building and chatted with the other competitors, media, and Chinese who were present. Everyone took pictures with us and La Girafe, and we were happy to cooperate and pose for them.

Finally, we were given updated weather information and reluctantly left this historic place for Wuhan, our next fuel stop, with Jim at the controls.

8

Kunming to Wuhan

Friday, March 6, 1987

In short order we were back in the air, having filed a flight plan to Wuhan. We departed at 16:56. The routing was simply A-81 direct to Wuhan (WUH) and would take about four hours.

During the first half of the trip, we observed the Chinese countryside. Again, the landscapes were varied and interesting. We flew over dams and reservoirs, reminiscent of the San Luis Reservoir area in California, strange little hill formations, rougher ranges, and some areas where it appeared that the hills and valleys were in straight lines, like corrugated paper.

Many small villages were interspersed in the less-hilly areas and around the lower hills. We were flying at 9,000 feet, which was low enough that we did not need to use oxygen. The sun was shining and the visibility was tremendous.

As night approached, the weather became progressively worse, and we began to pick up indications of thunderstorm activity on the storm-scope. The dots indicating convective activity were quite numerous to the east and south. We entered the clouds, and it became solid IFR as we approached Wuhan.

As we arrived over Wuhan, the controller, in broken English, vectored us to the runway in a nonstandard approach. The published approach called for an NDB (nondirectional beacon—actually two ADF) approach. Also, the approaches were not precise.

Jim flew as instructed, but when we were able to see the runway, it was almost directly to the right side of us. He did a "go-round," circling the airport again, and this time, he aimed slightly to the right and made an uneventful landing.

It was night and had been raining when we landed in Wuhan, at about 21:00, and it was extremely cold. Before we could get out of our airplane, a young attendant asked, "Can you fly in freezing conditions?" He repeated his question before we could respond.

Jim told him that we would like to go to the restroom before we tackled such a weighty question, so he showed us to the terminal where we entered through an unmarked door.

The room was full of high-ranking military men who stared at us in amazement. I am sure they wondered what we foreigners were doing there in the middle of the night. There also were people there to greet us, including two Chinese women, one of whom spoke English in order to greet me in my language and escort me to the restroom, without even being asked. It also was a hole in the floor, but this time at least it was inside the terminal building. Also, my guide disappeared for a moment and returned with toilet paper.

This terminal appeared to be used often and, in fact, there were many people there in other rooms, apparently waiting for commercial flights. Older men were seated in one dimly lit room, which obviously was the VIP lounge, or the closest thing to a VIP lounge in the egalitarian People's Republic of China.

After we had visited the facilities, we sat down and a young Chinese lady brought us cups of hot tea. We were given bad news, which confirmed what we already knew. There were numerous thunderstorms around the area, and the freezing level was quite low.

Because of the uncertainty of the weather, Jim told the young man who was assigned to help us that he wanted to go to the Met (weather) office to look at the weather depiction charts himself. This was highly unusual, he said, but he led Jim there anyway.

飞 行 天 气 预 报 表
FLIGHT WEATHER FORECAST BULLETIN

编号SERIAL № _12_   198_7_. _3. 6._

航线自 ROUTE FROM _Wuhan_   经过 VIA _Chenchow_   到 TO _Peking_

机型 TYPE OF AIRCRAFT _N6113√_   机号 AIRCRAFT IDENTIFICATION ____   预计起飞时间 ESTIMATED TIME OF DEPARTURE ____

发布预报气象台 ISSUED BY _Wuhan_   气象台 METEOROLOGICAL OFFICE   发布预报时间 ISSUED AT _1400_（北京时间 PEKING TIME）

航线及著陆和备降机场天气预报 ROUTE AND AERODROME (TERMINAL AND ALTERNATE) WEATHER FORECAST:

航线 ROUTE: 有效时间自 VALID FROM _0700_（GMT）到 TO _1600_（GMT）   _13ᵐ_   _1400ᵐ_

Wuhan to Peking Cloudy 5/8 Ac base 4000m top 6000m 7/8 Sc base
1000 m top 2700 m Pass yellow river 8/8 Ac
base 3000 m top 5400 m
There is slight turbulence.

Lcl +CB base 1000 m top 7000 m thunderstom

著陆和备降机场 AERODROME (TERMINAL AND ALTERNATE) 有效时间自 VALID FROM _0700_ (GMT) 到 _1500_ (GMT)

Surface wind 160/3 m/s VIS 5 KM Fu
WX no significant weather cloud 6/8 Ac base 2700m
6 ci base 6900 m slight turbulence

各层高空风与温度预报 UPPER WINDS AND TEMPERATURES FORECAST:

航 段 SECTOR	3000 米 M 向(度)DIRECTION (DEGS TRUE) 速(公里/时)VELOCITY(KM/HR)		温度(摄氏) TEMPERATURE(°C)	3600 米 M 向(度)DIRECTION (DEGS TRUE) 速(公里/时)VELOCITY(KM/HR)		温度(摄氏) TEMPERATURE(°C)	5400 米 M 向(度)DIRECTION (DEGS TRUE) 速(公里/时)VELOCITY(KM/HR)		温度(摄氏) TEMPERATURE(°C)
Wuhan to Chenchow	220	35	0	240	40	-3	370	70	-15
Chenchow to Peking (Zhengzhou)	270	40	-4	270	40	-7	250	80	-15

航线上天气实况 ENROUTE WEATHER:

Wuhan Flight Weather Forecast Bulletin.

Surprisingly, an older man was working in the Met office who spoke some English. It was soon apparent that the thunderstorms were to the east of Wuhan in the Shanghai area, and there were icing conditions between Wuhan and Beijing. It appeared that the storms were dissipating, so we made the decision to go on. We already had been refueled.

The freezing level was so low that it would be easy to climb above it to avoid icing. We were told that we would have to climb to 19,500 feet, which would have stretched our remaining oxygen supply severely. One of the race teams did stay the night in Wuhan, however, because they could not climb to even 13,000 feet and feared there would be icing at that level.

On returning to the airplane, Jim found me engrossed in a weighty conversation with two Chinese ladies who spoke surprisingly good English. They were curious about what we were doing there in the middle of their country in the middle of the night.

We said our goodbyes and departed.

9

Wuhan to Beijing

Friday, March 6, 1987

The time was 22:20. We departed Wuhan and were able to fly at 13,500 feet, which was lower than the 19,000 we had been advised might be required, with only Jim, who was flying this leg, using the oxygen. The night was clear after the first 50 or so miles, and we experienced no icing whatsoever.

The Chinese weather forecaster was extremely accurate, and we could see the thunderstorm activity on the stormscope. As predicted, the storms were in the Shanghai area. In fact, we learned the next day that a tornado had touched down in Shanghai, killing three people, injuring many others, and causing a considerable amount of property damage.

We were above the freezing level. Earlier, the Piper Comanche *Le Havre–Normandie*, flown by Michel Cogan-Portnoi and Yves Cressent, did pick up ice, but they were flying at a lower flight level than our 13,500 feet. Again, we were flying on A-81 direct to Beijing.

According to the charts, there were sufficient navigational aids between Wuhan and Beijing, and we had anticipated that there would be VORs and ADFs all along the route, so there would be few problems with navigation. Not true.

For the 600 nautical miles between Wuhan and Beijing, only one rather lazy NDB (Weixian-JX) was working, and it was not working well. None of the VORs located between Wuhan and Beijing were working, as they had been turned off, we were told, because of a lack of electricity. Therefore, we navigated with a watch and compass, having no idea what our ground speed was, although we knew that we had some headwinds.

It was dark, as there was cloud cover, so no moon or stars above and few, if any, lights from the ground. On occasion we would see a small village, but it was not as well lit as one would expect a populated area to be.

We learned later that there is a real power shortage, and for this reason the villages are principally dark, and the navigational aids are US (Unserviceable). Our Sat Nav was working from time to time, and this gave us a check on our heading and position, but it had never been programmed correctly to give us our ground speed.

The dearth of nav aids caused one unfortunate incident. We later learned that an American aircraft, the *Vail Snail*, captained by Chuck Rosenquist of Vail, Colorado, had navigational problems. He somehow missed Beijing and found himself approximately 90 miles north of Beijing, lost, and headed for the Russian (or Manchurian) border.

Fortunately, the race director, Bernard Lamy, was approaching Beijing in one of the organization's aircraft when he became aware of the problem. He circled the Beijing airport, and Chuck spoke with him and a couple of other competitors who had not yet reached Beijing. By the strength of the various transmissions, Bernard triangulated Chuck's position and vectored him back toward Beijing, where he subsequently was picked up by Beijing radar and vectored in for a safe landing.

When we were approximately 120 nautical miles from the Beijing airport, we experienced our first real problem of the race. This was where we found ourselves flying through a dark night, not knowing whether we were going to crash and die or live and be able to see our family again.

Our engine began to miss noticeably. It coughed, sputtered, and choked. It continued to run but missed regularly. Since we had nowhere else to land, we continued our approach to Beijing. We were out of radio contact with Wuhan by then, and not yet in contact with Beijing or any other control. For some time, we could not contact anyone, but finally we contacted another race aircraft on the 123.45 common frequency and told them of our problem. They relayed the information to Beijing.

The engine kept erratically chugging along, and fortunately the airplane kept flying. We finally began to receive the ILS DME for runway 36R in Beijing. As we were tracking the ILS inbound, we advised the controller of our problem and requested a straight-in approach. We definitely were not interested in receiving a series of vectors.

For some strange reason, Jim remembered a line from the 1917 US Flying Corp Rules of the Air: "Machines with dead motors have the right of way over all others." That was certainly appropriate in our situation.

Suddenly, we heard the old familiar voice of Patrick, the air traffic controller from the French technical team, on the radio, and he gave us the straight-in approach that we had requested. We remained high until we had the runway made and landed without further incident, although the engine continued missing. Just to be safe, the tower had called out the fire trucks and rescue vehicles, but, fortunately, they were not needed this night.

We landed at about 01:20. We made it and breathed a huge sigh of relief.

Although we landed safely, we knew there were problems with the engine. Jim went to the airport the next day with Hubert Rault, the French mechanic from the technical team traveling with the organization, and they found that one of the spark plugs was totally burned up and the others were fouled.

The Chinese aviation gasoline was about the color of strong beer, and though it was supposed to be 90 octane, it obviously was not. Whether our engine and fuel problems were caused by the octane level of the Chinese gasoline or impurities in the fuel we had purchased, we will never know. Nevertheless, Hubert cleaned our spark plugs. In fact, most of the airplanes needed to have their spark plugs cleaned before we left Beijing.

10

Beijing

Saturday, March 7, 1987

While flying across China, we thought about the history of this great country and were thrilled to have the opportunity to now join in the stream of that history, even if it was in a rather insignificant fashion when compared with past events.

The People's Republic of China has been in power since 1949, when Mao Tse-tung expelled the Nationalist government of Chiang Kai-shek. The Nationalist leadership, including Chiang Kai-shek and part of his army, fled to Formosa (today's Taiwan), where the Nationalists remain in power today. The Nationalists still claim to be the only legitimate government of all of China, and the People's Republic of China claims Taiwan.

We landed in Beijing at approximately 1:20 a.m. local time. The Chronopost team had landed just shortly before us. They were waiting with Claude Jaubert from the technical team for the bus to arrive and take us to our hotel. We waited approximately fifteen minutes in the freezing cold for the bus, which had taken other competitors to the hotel and was returning to fetch us.

When it finally arrived, we were so anxious to get inside where it was warm that we did not unload our luggage from the airplane. It was too cold and dark. We took only an overnight bag and a change of clothes for the next day.

While in Beijing, we were guests at the Holiday Inn Lido Beijing. It was a modern hotel located approximately halfway between the center of the city and the international airport. The contrast between new and old was evident in the parts of China we visited, but especially in Beijing. Many apartment buildings were under construction. These, together with the modern office buildings and hotels, made the city resemble downtown Warsaw (though not Paris or a modern American city).

We were exhausted and slept in until approximately 11:00 a.m. We had lunch, and then Jim and I walked outside and toured a couple of blocks around the hotel. It was extremely cold, so our walk was not long.

After that, we attended the press conference in the open bar above the hotel's entrance. It was interesting and well attended. During the press conference, Bernard, who usually spoke English perfectly, referred to the "public" on several occasions, though he mispronounced it as sounding more like "pubic." Jim and David (from the Cathay team) exchanged exasperated expressions and afterward approached Bernard to explain to him the difference in pronunciation.

Bernard said, "Well, you should have stopped me!"

To which Jim said, "How could we stop you when we didn't know what you were going to say?"

I was interviewed by someone from Beijing Radio. First a fellow interviewed me, but evidently his tape machine was not functioning properly, so a woman completed the interview. This was one of many interviews, and it seemed as though I was always on the radio or television.

After the press conference, Jim and I, plus some of the other competitors, went to the airport to check the airplanes and obtain our luggage. When we arrived at the airfield, we found that the race airplanes were all surrounded by armed guards.

Since their instructions were to guard the airplanes—no exceptions—they would not allow us to go to our own airplanes. We talked to the initial group of guards for some time, trying to explain as well as we could (in sign language, as they did not speak English, and we did not speak Chinese) that we needed our luggage and to check our airplanes, but this was universally denied. We walked down the row to another guard who was standing a short distance away and closer to our airplanes, but he was equally adamant that none of us could go to our airplanes.

I then walked toward a third guard and tried with all of my persuasive powers and sign language to explain to him in logical English why I needed to go to the airplane, indicating that it was our airplane, my clothes were there, and I had nothing else to wear.

In clear Chinese, he explained to me that I would not be allowed to do this. He seemed to be a nice young man, and I did convince him, somehow, that he should check with the chief, or whoever was in charge, as I was sure that someone must have the authority to allow me to go to my airplane. Finally seeming to understand, he agreed to check and walked back to the main group of guards.

When he was a safe distance away, I casually began walking quickly toward our airplane, hoping that no one would notice. I was almost there when the last guard I had chatted with began yelling and running toward me. I ignored him, of course. I was not sure that he was yelling at me, and I did not want to turn around to see. I simply walked faster. I knew that he had a rifle and heard what I thought was a slap of the rifle stock being taken off his shoulder, smacked into his hand, and pointed at me.

Someone, evidently one of the other competitors, yelled, "Judy, stop!" But I assumed that this nice young guard would not shoot me in the back, since this would create not only a mess, but an international incident. I did not think he would do this simply to prevent me from going to our airplane, so I ignored the warnings and continued to walk faster toward our airplane.

Just as I arrived at our airplane and opened the door, the rifle-carrying guard also arrived and indicated that I was to close the door. I simply pretended that I did not understand, explained again in perfect English what I needed to get from the airplane, and began removing things.

Since he was still yelling and motioning to me, I handed him some charts that were on the front seat and said, "Hold these for me." Evidently, he was surprised and did not know exactly how else to react, so he took the charts I had handed him and held them for me. I began to remove the suitcases when another guard appeared, so I handed him a suitcase. He

The Chinese guard at the airport who wouldn't
allow me to go to my own airplane and chased me
across the tarmac with his weapon drawn.

apparently was the chief and had decided that it was all right for the other pilots and me to go to our airplanes.

We helped mend relations by taking pictures of everyone. All of the security guards wanted their pictures taken—some with me and some with just the airplane. The guard who had chased me across the tarmac was a sweet, baby-faced young man, and I took a Polaroid picture and gave it to him.

As I left, he said in heavily accented English, "Goodbye. See you later." He was so sweet. I knew that he wouldn't shoot me. I thought that perhaps this was one occasion when it was an advantage to being a woman.

Jim had been talking to some of the other competitors and learned that the Cathay Pacific team in *Spirit of Hong Kong* had some problems with one of their engines missing, also due to the fuel in Wuhan, and some of the other airplanes had dirty spark plugs. Everyone doubted that the octane level was sufficiently high.

Although two airplanes—ours and Rosenquist's, the *Vail Snail*—had problems, all of the other competitors landed safely the day before without incident except for *Bio-France Elevage*, which had stayed in Wuhan for the night and flew in the next day. It was the only airplane that could not climb high enough to stay out of the icing conditions.

In the early evening, we attended a reception at the beautiful residence of the French ambassador and his wife, and afterward we had a delicious Chinese dinner at the hotel. Jean Le Ber, Jean-Michel Masson, and Marie Desne, of the Le Ber–Masson team; Umberto Sala, the sponsor of his airplane of the same name; Fabio Isman from the Italian newspaper *Il Messaggero*; Jean-Claude Kaufmann of the organization; and Allen Funch and his guest Annette Newman sat at our table.

We drank all the available wine, sent the staff to the cellar several times, and even though they said they had no wine, they always found more. We closed the place and then went to the disco and danced until about 2:00 a.m. to good old American rock music. It was a great disco—as good as any we had seen anywhere.

The winner of the Paris-to-Beijing half of the race was *Microjet-Mammouth*, a Wassmer 421 piloted by Raymond Michel. The copilot was Christian Laloé, and the photojournalist was Rémi Grasset. This was the smallest aircraft in the race, but evidently had the longest range. The crew was secretive about the range of the aircraft.

Second place was awarded to the TDK aircraft, a Piper Malibu piloted by François Garçon. The copilot was Patrick Ducommun, and the photojournalist was Alain Théveneau. Third place was nailed down by *AAAAA-Rent-A-Space,* the Cessna 421C piloted by James (Jim) Knuppe. The crew was composed of Steve Picatti and Marc Mosier, our first contact for the race. All three were pilots.

On March 9, 1987, Jim Knuppe filed a formal protest against the Wassmer with the organization. He amended his protest on March 10, 1987, and sent it off to the F.A.I. jury, together with his check for 1,000 French francs, which was about $350. Jim asked the judges to make the following findings:

1) The mircojet [sic] was illegally admitted as specified under Chapter II, article 2-4. (The aircraft's V-ref is 132 knots; 140 knots is required.)
2) The mircojet [sic]) was illegally accepted in violation of Chapter III, article 3-6, second paragraph, last sentence.
3) To find that there should be no exceptions from providing a copy of the aircraft's manual spelling out "The aircraft's max. takeoff weight, the power, true airspeed, with 65% power at optimum altitude and the same copy must be sent to the air race committee for approval as required in the rules."
4) To find that the spirit of the race was violated and that the crew (participants) were not properly notified as required under article 3-7 Chapter III. That the mircojet [sic] was accepted as a participant without presenting a page from its manual, but by test flight only and was given its V-ref speed based on this one test only.
5) To find under article 6-1, method of classification that the last paragraph specifies without exception that each crew competing will furnish the copy of power settings at 65% of his flight manual.

Jim Knuppe later paid the balance of the funds required to perfect his protest. The protest caused a great deal of grumbling among the French participants, and, finally, Bernard Lamy had to intervene.

At one of our briefings, he announced that he had some comments for the French-speaking participants, and the words were not for the American crews. Then, quite uncharacteristically, he spoke for some time in French. A rough translation was that Bernard informed them that Jim Knuppe had a right to file the protest and that no one was to hassle him over the incident.

The fact of the matter is that Jim had a good point. It had become quite obvious that *Microjet-Mammouth* was capable of flying much faster and farther than advertised. Jim and I were never concerned about such matters. We were totally wrapped up in the adventure of the trip, and finishing positions were of no importance to us. The way that the race was hand-icapped prevented us from finishing well anyway, so this was never a consideration. We were just happy to be participating.

According to the Cessna owner's manual, the optimum speed and altitude for our T210 was 181 knots at 16,000 feet. Since we could rarely obtain oxygen, we were unable to fly at that altitude, thus we could not achieve 181 knots on a consistent basis. That is the reason that the non-turbo aircraft (310s, Trinidads, and the Microjet) had such an advantage. Their speed for handicap purposes was computed at a much lower alti-tude, and, of course, they could consistently attain it. This is not a matter of sour grapes—at least for *Winged Quest*—because, "Frankly my dear, we didn't give a damn!"

Sunday, March 8, 1987
THE FORBIDDEN CITY

The early wake-up was difficult, as we all felt rather rocky after the eve-ning of wine and disco partying. A bus took us to the Forbidden City.

In the center of Beijing is Tian'anmen Square. Here, Tian'anmen Gate is the north-south access to the city of Beijing. During the Ming and Qing dynasties, it was the south and principal gate of the Imperial Palace, and it was on each side of Tian'anmen Square that the Chinese government established their offices.

On October 1, 1949, Mao Tse-tung claimed the formal establishment of the People's Republic of China from this square. Since that time, a large portrait of Mao has hung over the central archway of the Tian'anmen Gate, with large plaques on each side. To the east, the plaque reads "Long live the People's Republic of China" and to the west, "Long live the unity of the Peoples of the World." China's national emblem hangs over Mao's portrait in the eaves of the gate tower.

To enter the palace museum through its present gate, the Merid-ian Gate (Wumen), it is necessary to first pass through Tian'anmen. We drove by the big square and Mao's tomb. A big rally was due to begin, celebrating the International Day of Women. I would have liked very much to attend the rally; however, we were taken to the entrance to the

Entrance to the Forbidden City.

Forbidden City where we spent the morning walking from one beautiful courtyard to the next.

The Forbidden City was, for hundreds of years, the home of the emperor, his many wives, thousands of eunuchs, and others. At one point, we calculated how often each of the wives would enjoy a visit with the emperor, if he visited one per day. We figured she would see him about once every twenty-five years.

At the Forbidden City's entrance, five or six rows of bicycles extended as far as we could see. Well-tended and shaped shrubbery surrounded the Forbidden City, and you enter via a bridge across a wide moat. An impressive-looking lion statue guards the bridge.

One of the first courtyards is large, and evidently a place where many ceremonies were held. There are two rows of steps at the courtyard's far end, ascending to a large building with columns across the front and an Asian-style roof. Between the two sets of steps is a ramp made of intricately carved stone.

Around the edges of the courtyard are many large urns. These contained oil, which was set aflame for light. There is a large stork sculpture and other large sculptures such as a lion and a turtle. In one of the courtyards rises a beautiful, brilliantly colored wall. Depicting seven dragons, it is known as the Seven Dragon Wall. It is impressive.

There is a theater, approximately three stories high, and inside is an open area where one can look down from the third balcony. Near the Forbidden City's exit or back entrance, a few buildings house a collection of objects that are quite stunning and intricate. These include costumes, paintings, prints, elaborate gold work, jade, dishes, sculpture, and jewelry.

After leaving the Forbidden City, we went to the Beijing Hotel for lunch. Again, we had a traditional Chinese meal, with the dishes placed on a lazy Susan and served family style. One fellow (I do not know his name, and he was not a competitor, but we believe he was with the Italian team) broke into song spontaneously at the beginning of the meal, and I filmed him with my video camera.

TEMPLE OF HEAVEN

After lunch, we went to the Temple of Heaven. This is an old temple with surrounding buildings, where in previous centuries the Chinese worshiped and offered sacrifices to the gods for a good harvest. Evidently the sacrifices were primarily grain and occasionally small animals. There were no human sacrifices.

Again, the buildings, primarily the reddish color of new brick, were ornately decorated with colorful tiles on the inside ceilings and just under the roof on the outside, and ornate carvings decorate the stonework over the doors, archways, steps, and walls. The roofs seem to be made of tiles. It is all striking.

While we were in the temple, the King of Tanzania and his entourage came in. We saw them again outside, walking down the wide pathway to the other buildings and outdoor pavilion.

Many Chinese people were there, not simply tourists, and outside of the main temple two girls played some type of game that seemed to be a cross between badminton and ping pong. Many young children were present, playing with kites and each other.

The area around the Temple of Heaven is higher than the rest of the city, and from the round, open area where the ceremonies were held, one has a good view of the city of Beijing.

There was a great deal of new construction with high cranes everywhere. We saw many new high-rise buildings, and it appeared that the older, dilapidated areas were being torn down. Some of them seemed to have been there for centuries, and the old brick walls, some of which were now in a state of disrepair, had obviously seen a great deal of history. It was sad to see so many old buildings being destroyed.

Temple of Heaven.

OFFICIAL DINNER

That evening, the official ceremonial dinner was held at the Great Hall of Parliament. This is a large, ornate room with a stage, and evidently a historic place, having been used for many official functions. There were many Chinese officials and dignitaries there, including Deng Xiaoping's son, who was in a wheelchair, having been pushed from a second-story window during the upheaval of the Cultural Revolution. (Deng Xiaoping, the paramount leader, had planned to attend, but was ill that night.)

Seated at the table with Jim and me was a colonel from the American Embassy; Jim Knuppe, the pilot of the Cessna 421; and a number of Chinese officials, including one whom we had met in Kunming. Another of the officials was the Minister of Public Security. He had requested that he be placed at our table, and he gave us a gift of some pictures.

At the end of the dinner, which began at 6:00 p.m., a fairly early hour for us, there were speeches in Chinese, English, and French. Patricia Lamy, Bernard's daughter, impressed all of us when she did a simultaneous translation from Mandarin Chinese to English, even though her native language is, of course, French.

Then the winners of the Paris-to-Beijing portion of the race were presented. As the first-place Microjet team (flying the Wassmer) and the second-place TDK team were called to the stage, the TDK team brought a bamboo birdcage with a dove onto the stage as well. After the awards were presented, the dove was released as a symbol of peace and goodwill. The dove flew away and up onto a small railing around the balcony.

As Jim Knuppe, with Steve Picatti and Marc Mosier, were presented their third-place trophy, Jim thanked the Chinese official in Chinese. We were surprised, but later learned that he had studied Chinese as a child. His efforts stirred some applause. He then accepted the award in English on behalf of himself, his crew, and the people of the United States.

Jim and I gave gifts from our sponsors of raisins, raisin hats, pins, T-shirts, address books, and almonds to the officials at our table. There were not enough gifts to go around, but by dividing up the large pack of raisins into three individual packs (golden, regular, and chocolate-covered), there were sufficient gifts for everyone.

The next problem was how to decide which official was to get which gift. Jim and I solved this when the lazy Susan in the center of the table had been cleared of food and dishes. We described the gifts, told the officials at the table about our sponsors, and put each gift on the lazy Susan. We then played "spin the gifts" and encouraged each person to take a gift. No one wished to choose first, so we had to pick which official would have the first choice. The most diplomatic way I could think of was to simply start at my right and go around the table, which I did. The first official chose the raisin hat, and after removing his official hat, he put it on immediately. He was proud of his new hat, and, of course, we took his picture.

The T-shirt from International English Institute was the next to be chosen, and then the other gifts disappeared rapidly. The session ended with the various officials trading the three types of raisins back and forth. "I'll give you a chocolate for a regular," although this was all in Chinese, so we could only guess at what they were saying. Our gifts were a big hit.

Shortly thereafter, a man came over to our table to meet us, because he knew we were from the United States. He told us that he had worked with the CAAC (Civil Aviation Administration of China) during World War II, bringing supplies and working with the Flying Tigers out of Kunming. He said that he knew General Chennault well, and every Sunday they would "lift a few beers and party." He said that he was good friends with all of the members of the Flying Tigers, and he seemed to be proud of his connection with them.

We were advised that he was now a hero of the Chinese government because, even though he had gone to Taiwan with the Nationalist Chinese during the revolution, he had subsequently stolen one of their jets and flown it back to China. We took a video of him and then filmed the other officials at our table as well.

There were many toasts, and we were given some type of Chinese wine or liquor that was extremely strong, along with our beer and regular wine. This beverage was served in a small glass. It appears that when one has an important toast, one drinks this beverage, and *chugs* the whole glass. Even though the glass was only about an inch deep, there was no way that I could drink even one of them, let alone more, and I even had trouble taking more than a polite sip. Fortunately, the Chinese forgave me—probably because I am a woman—but Jim was not so fortunate.

One of the Chinese officials toasted, emptied his glass, and showed the empty glass to Jim. This was obviously an indication that Jim was to do the same. He protested, as he is not a big drinker, and especially not of strong liquor, but the colonel from the American Embassy said that it would be polite and further said, "Do it for your country!"

Therefore, Jim drank the whole glass in one swallow and showed the empty glass to the Chinese official who had toasted him. Subsequently, each of the other officials made a toast, each time drinking the whole glass and showing the empty glass to Jim, who had to do the same. After the first couple of glasses, Jim did not protest as much, and there was a great round of toasting.

Jim does not remember the end of the dinner, going back to the hotel, or getting into bed. He also does not remember that I took a video of him in bed talking about the dinner, which he had just had in Phoenix! He was quite happy.

Monday, March 9, 1987

Zhou Baochen called. When I answered the phone, he said, "You're here! I saw you on television when you arrived in Kunming, so I have been following you and found you here."

He did not have a lot of time, but he wanted to see us. Baochen had been a visiting scholar at California State University–Fresno about two years before, and we had met him at a dinner that he prepared at the home of our friend Anne Speake. Afterward, we had invited him to our home for Thanksgiving dinner. He was now the vice president of the China International Travel Service in Beijing.

Jim had gone to the airport to refuel the airplane and meet Hubert, the mechanic, to check it, so I met Baochen at 11:00 a.m., and we drove in his beautiful Lincoln with a chauffeur to a lovely little street in an older part of the city with antique shops on each side. The shops appeared quite old but restored, and they were beautifully decorated.

Baochen said that this area had been recently restored, and he thought it would become a popular area with tourists, though most people were not aware of it yet. The clerks in the antique shops knew who I was, and they would disappear into the back and bring out their family, who would all smile and move their arms in a flying gesture.

When I expressed surprise to Baochen, he told me that I had been appearing on Chinese TV, as well as in the newspapers, and that "500 million people in China know who you are."

I wanted to find an antique doll for my doll collection, but the only antique dolls were porcelain. I found one of an old man with a great expression carrying a fish, and Baochen checked to see whether it was authentic. He advised me that it was approximately 110 years old and in good condition, so I purchased it. I also bought an interesting old vase.

Baochen had to go on to another meeting, so I asked that he drop me off at the Friendship Store so that I could do more shopping before I returned to the hotel.

The Friendship Store is similar to a large department store. There are areas where food, drugs (both modern and traditional), household supplies, office equipment, clothing, jewelry, and more are sold. I spent about an hour touring the store and then began buying things. At first, the store was not crowded, but soon there were many more of the race competitors there, as well as more local people, and the store became crowded.

I was trying on fur hats, not only for myself, but for Jim and our two sons, Kevin and Edward. There were a couple of other competitors around, and we were discussing sizes, trying on the hats and clowning back and forth.

Soon, Dominique Simon, the Chronopost photographer who initially had not spoken to us, was laughing and trying on hats with me. I had seen him in other areas of the store, and it seemed that we kept running into each other.

Here it was unavoidable that I say something to him, as I turned around and we were face-to-face, so I said something in French. He gave me a big smile (probably the first of the trip) and started talking and laughing and joking as though we were longtime friends. Evidently, speaking French to him broke the ice, and we were now friends. He even helped carry my bags, which were becoming rather numerous, to the credit card line.

One cannot pay for purchases at the counter, but, rather, the purchases are delivered to a little booth, and one takes a credit card to the booth to pay. This is no problem when the store is not crowded, but if there are many people, the line can become long. Since all of the credit cards were checked through a telephone confirmation service, the process can take a long time.

I next took all of my purchases to the shipping area, which was next door to the store. They assured me that everything would be shipped and would arrive in about a month. The shipping cost quite a bit, however, so anything I had saved by buying items at a low price was lost to shipping charges.

I was going to catch a cab back to the hotel when Jim and Jean-Michel arrived. Since Jim is known as an avid nonshopper, I was surprised, but accompanied him back into the Friendship Store. We bought a few more things and then returned to the hotel. We were supposed to meet with a publicist with the Holiday Inn at 5:00 p.m., but it was already 5:20 when we arrived at the hotel, and we were supposed to catch the bus at 5:30 for dinner. Therefore, we simply ran to the room, changed clothes, and ran to the bus.

PEKIN DUCK DINNER

We took a bus to the restaurant where we were to have an authentic Pekin duck dinner. The bus could not drive us all the way to the restaurant, as it was in a narrow alley, so it stopped in a parking area and we walked down a street, past many artsy shops, and turned down the alley.

The door to the restaurant was not large, and it seemed that we were entering a side door of a building rather than into the front door of a restaurant. However, the sign over the door assured us that we were in the right place. We went upstairs and passed several other rooms of various sizes where banquets were being served, down the hall, to our own banquet room.

We were seated at round tables, each of which was set for ten people, with a lazy Susan in the center. We sat with Jean Le Ber, Jean-Michel Masson, Gilles Rousseau, François Dabin, Marie Desne, and a woman from Miami. Also, Allen and Annette Newman, a friend of Allen's and manager of his shopping center, who had come to meet us, were seated with us.

The American woman from Miami was traveling alone. At the hotel, she had requested that she be allowed to join our group for the dinner, since she was not able to go to such a restaurant alone. They only served groups.

Tuesday, March 10, 1987
THE GREAT WALL OF CHINA

We left the hotel early in three buses and headed to the Great Wall. The Chinese countryside was interesting and full of contrasts. There were a few modern buses, trucks, and cars, but the main modes of transportation were mostly horses or mules, with some people pulling wagons and carts along the roadway.

The landscape was fairly brown and the trees were bare, though in spring, summer, and fall, this would probably be a beautiful area. We shortly left the flat plains surrounding Beijing and began winding through the foothills, which gradually became higher and more rugged. The road was good, and much of it appeared to be fairly new. For a while, a railroad track paralleled the road to our right, and soon we saw a steam locomotive pushing some cars up the grade and through a tunnel.

The Great Wall of China.

As we drove along, we could see portions of the Great Wall from time to time. We drove through an area populated with little shops and a camel (for photo taking), and we stopped. We had arrived at the Great Wall.

It is said that the Great Wall was built by the Emperor Qin Shi Huang in approximately 221 BC, although some sections were erected as early as the fifth century BC. Qin is called the "Unifier of China," since in 211 BC, his armies conquered the Chinese kingdoms that had existed, each with its own separate defensive walls. He ordered the demolition of the walls separating the kingdoms and rebuilt the new "Great Wall" to protect the northern frontiers.

The wall, which follows the contours of the land, was originally more than 3,000 miles long. More than 300,000 men worked for two years to complete the wall, which has a pounded-earth interior with stone facings and a stone roadway along the top. The top roadway is wide enough to allow five or six horses to stand abreast, and it was formerly used to take soldiers, munitions, food, and supplies to various locations along the frontier.

Many men lost their lives working on the wall, and their remains form a part of the interior. The wall had fallen into disrepair, but it now had been restored in several places. The nearest section to Beijing is approximately 40 miles from the city and is named Badaling.

Jim, me, and La Girafe on the Great Wall of China on a bitterly cold day.

Our perceptions of the Great Wall were instantly dispelled. I thought that one simply climbed a flight of steps to the top of the Great Wall, which would be relatively flat, then looked over the other side, to the right, to the left, and that was all there would be to it. Wrong!

The Great Wall is miles and miles of walkways and steps, sometimes nearly vertical, following the hills and dipping into the valleys, separating what was old China from the invading Mongols or enemies to the north. As one looks out across the plains to the north, it is easy to imagine the hordes attacking the fortified wall and the many lives and lifetimes that have been a part of this place.

It is not a simple walk but a true aerobic exercise to venture even a short distance along the wall. From the point where we entered, in a valley, there was a view of what appeared to be the high point in the wall off to the left. We decided that we would at least try to accomplish this point. I had brought La Girafe with me, and also my video and 35mm cameras. I wore my red race jacket and the fur hat that I had purchased at the Friendship Store.

I soon found that I needed less to carry and more to wear. It was absolutely freezing, and the wind carried the chill through our jackets and blew off my hat at every opportunity. I not only had to carry my two cameras

With a Chinese guard and La Girafe on the Great Wall.

and the giraffe, but also had to hold my hat on as well. It was so cold on the wall that the focus on my still camera froze, and I had a difficult time taking pictures the rest of the day. Most of my pictures are blurred.

La Girafe was a great hit on the wall, as he had been in other places as well. Jean Le Ber posed with him and assisted him to walk up a particularly steep flight of stairs. He also posed with a passing tourist, an old Chinese lady with a beautiful round face, and some friendly Chinese guards.

When we arrived at the high point on the wall that we had seen from below, the view was worth the arduous climb. More miles of the wall spread out in front of us, as a challenge we did not accept. The bus was due to leave shortly, so we returned. At least the return trip was easier, since we were now traveling mostly downhill.

The bus took us down through a narrower, winding, older road that was quite rough in places, to a restaurant and touristy little square in a remote area. The food was adequate, and we were all happy to be inside and warm. There was a cardboard figure of a horse with a headless warrior astride, and several of our group, Jim included, paid a small sum to be photographed "dashing off to battle." This was a particularly interesting picture to me because Jim does not ride horses—ever.

Jim on horseback, charging off to battle when we stopped at a little square for a meal.

MING TOMBS

We next went to the Ming Tombs. Sixteen Ming emperors ruled from 1368 to 1644, the period of the Ming Dynasty. The tombs of thirteen of these emperors are buried in an area about 50 kilo-meters from Beijing. At Dingling, the tomb buildings had been renovated and the tomb of the fourteenth emperor, Wan Li, was excavated.

The area is beautiful and serene, surrounded by foothills and then mountains. One enters through a big gate and proceeds along the Avenue of the Animals, lined by huge stone lions, elephants, camels, horses, and other animals. There are also human figures, evidently repre-senting the funeral bearers.

The tombs at Dingling are underground and consist of five rooms. There is first a front hall, then a central hall with three marble imperial thrones, oil lamps, incense burners, candlesticks, and vases. Adjacent to this hall are two side chambers, each containing a marble coffin platform. The rear hall contains three platforms used to support coffins. There are also red lacquer chests.

Between the first chamber and the middle chamber are two six-inch-thick marble doors with a locking stone. The stone fits into a slot in the floor and would slide down to lock the door from the inside once it had been closed.

ITALIAN AMBASSADOR'S RECEPTION

That evening, we went to a reception at the Italian Embassy. The ambassador and his wife were friendly and gracious. He told us that his first post as a diplomat was in New York when he was still a bachelor, and he had enjoyed that immensely. He also said that he had served in San Francisco when he was "a little boy" and loved it. The embassy was like a museum, with beautiful old tapestries, paintings, chandeliers, and other items that he must have collected from around the world.

We later were taken by bus to an area in downtown Beijing where we were to see an acrobatic show. The bus could not drive close to the theater, as the streets were narrow. We had to walk a long way past restaurants and crowded shops. The show was in an old ornate, but small, theater.

A few people sat in a balcony. There were many Chinese present, as well as our group, and the show was under way when we entered. There were balancing acts, gymnasts, and magicians. One of the magicians invited Jorge de Brito, our Chronopost friend who was to be a member of the team on the return trip to Paris, onto the stage, and put on a good act.

The magician told Jorge that when he counted to three, he should reach over and pull the front of his hair. They practiced this maneuver two or three times, and then the magician brought out a trunk. Jorge got into the trunk and examined it and then got out.

Next, a girl came onto the stage. She was placed in a large bag, and Jorge tied the knot to close the top of it. This bag was then put in the trunk, which was closed and locked, and then ropes were tied around it. The magician stood in front of the trunk, and a large cape was put around his shoulders, with the back covering the trunk. Only his head was showing.

He then counted, "one, two, three," and Jorge reached over to pull his hair as he had been directed. Instead, the magician ducked down, the girl popped up, and Jorge pulled her hair. The cape was removed, and the trunk was as it had been.

Jorge examined the ropes and locks, and, after removing them, opened the trunk. The large bag was still tied with the same bow Jorge had made, and he had some difficulty untying it. The magician was inside. We had no idea how the switch was accomplished. It was truly magic!

11

Beijing to Guangzhou

Wednesday, March 11, 1987

After a wonderful time in Beijing, we suffered an early wake-up on March 11, 1987. We were the first airplane to take off, leaving Beijing for Guangzhou at about 07:00 by old reliable (without nav aids) A-81. At least this time our airplane ran smoothly along this route.

Because of forecast headwinds, we filed for 9,000 feet, lower than we usually would have flown. The weather was clear but cold when we departed. After about two hours, the clear skies gave way to clouds, and we entered the eerie world of white-solid IFR. We were disappointed, as the landscape below fascinated us.

We had intended to fly direct from Beijing to Guangzhou. However, the headwinds were even stronger than forecasted and much too strong to fly to Guangzhou directly, so we decided to again stop in Wuhan, as we had done on the way from Kunming to Beijing, to obtain additional fuel. We hoped that the fuel would be good this time.

We could see on the stormscope that there were storms in addition to the headwinds between Wuhan and Guangzhou. On reaching Wuhan, the controller cleared us for the NDB approach to runway 36. This was the same runway where Jim had landed after a go-round on our way to Beijing.

feet	meters
650	200
1300	400
1950	600
2000	615
2500	769
2600	800
3000	923
3250	1000
3500	1077
4000	1231
5000	1538
6000	1846
6500	2000
7000	2154
7500	2308
8000	2461
8500	2615
9000	2770
9750	3000
10,000	3077
11,000	3385
12,000	3692
13,000 (13,500)	4000 (4153)

My handwritten conversion
table of feet to meters.

The weather around Wuhan was so foggy that we could not see the ground until we were about 500 feet above it. This time, I was flying, and even though I had my IFR rating, I had little experience flying "hard IFR."

This was a tricky NDB approach. Our airplane had one ADF, and this approach required two. As far as we knew, there were no airports in the United States that required two ADFs. With our one, we had to switch between the two frequencies.

The first time we descended to minimums we could not see the runway. I did a go-round and tried again. It seemed that the two-ADF approach guided us a little to the left of the runway, so I flew slightly right of the course. This time, when we got close enough to see the ground, the threshold of the runway was almost below us, but off to our right. I made a diving S turn and landed.

I thought to myself, "I see it, I land on it!" I could see the runway this time and did not want to go around again.

After refueling, this time hopefully with good fuel, we departed for Guangzhou at about 11:00. The Wuhan weather briefing revealed that thunderstorms were forecast for the route. We had filed for A-461 and 3,000 meters (9,750 feet) because of the winds. In China, all flight levels were given in meters.

We had a handwritten conversion table that allowed us to quickly convert meters to feet. We also had a conversion table for millibars (hectopascals) to inches of mercury. With Jim now flying, we departed in the clouds and virtually remained in the clouds for the entire flight.

Between Wuhan and Guangzhou, the storm activity increased. The flight was bumpy and occasionally we flew through rain squalls. About one hour out of Guangzhou, we began to receive strong thunderstorm activity on our stormscope. The thunderstorms were active across our entire route. They were moving north, but not fast enough for us to avoid them.

At first, we could fly around them because, with the controllers' blessing, we were permitted to deviate from the airway for storm avoidance purposes. However, for the last hour of the flight, this was no longer possible. The storm cells were too thick, and the ride became bumpy. We slowed the airplane to the maneuvering speed (139 knots indicated) and prepared for a very rough ride. There was no alternate airport close enough to provide a means of escape.

Jim Knuppe's Cessna 421C, *AAAAA-Rent-A-Space*, was slightly ahead of us and at a flight level above 180. During one period of time, we were out of contact with both Wuhan and Guangzhou control, so Marc Mosier, one of the crew, was relaying for us. Again, we requested that we be given permission to deviate from course to avoid the storm and were given permission to deviate 10 miles each side of the course.

We managed to avoid most of the storm, but we had to fly through the edge of one cloud, and while there was no electrical activity, there was a lot of hail. It continued for at least ten minutes and sounded as though someone was shooting rapid-fire BBs at our windshield. We were flying at an altitude of 3,200 meters (just over 10,500 feet), but Jim was having difficulty holding altitude, since we were often in an updraft.

The difference between the way we felt going through this terrible, turbulent weather was different from the way we had felt when our engine was missing between Wuhan and Beijing. At that time, we thought that our engine might stop at any minute and we might die. Here, our engine was humming along perfectly and its sound was reassuring to us. This was our cocoon that kept us safe from the tempest surrounding us. We were uncomfortable sometimes, but we trusted our airplane and felt safe and secure inside.

Finally, the stormscope displayed nothing but solid dots. It looked as though someone was practicing acupuncture on it. Sometimes the little green dots were so close together that they were simply a mass. Heavy rain began to pound the airplane, and we experienced severe turbulence. Marc indicated that they, too, were being tossed around. In fact, they suffered damage to the nose of their airplane from hail. We went through hail, but suffered no structural damage.

After the hail abated, we were still IFR. As we approached Guangzhou, the controller vectored us in to land on a nonstandard approach to runway 21, even though they had an ILS. We could hear the Caffè Lavazza team on the radio, and they seemed to be in some sort of trouble, so we thought we were being vectored in on a straight-in approach so that we could get out of their way and the controller could bring them in. The controller was also talking to a commercial airplane in Chinese, and the Hong Kong team, Hotel Echo, was also on the radio.

We were still in the clouds when we received his final vector and instruction to descend to 500 meters (about 1,640 feet). When the controller asked us, "Do you have the airport in sight?" we were still completely in the clouds and could see nothing.

"NO!" Jim replied, somewhat irritated that the controller did not know what the weather was at his own field.

There was silence for a minute, and Jim asked for further instructions. The controller did not respond right away. Nothing. Then he began talking rapidly in Chinese, either to someone else or to us, and then he loudly ordered us (in English): "Climb, climb to 620 meters! Very dangerous! Climb immediately, climb to 620 meters!"

We did so, and then he told us to turn to 315 degrees. His voice was still loud, high, and excited. Jim asked if we should make the turn to the right or to the left, and he did not respond; he just kept yelling at us to turn to 315 degrees and climb to 620 meters. Jim turned to the left. We reached 620 meters and advised the controller of this.

The controller continued talking to other traffic in Chinese. Finally, he vectored us in for an ILS approach to runway 3. We intercepted the glideslope and shot the approach. Visibility was minimum, if that, but Jim had no problem and landed without further incident at about 14:00.

The Caffè Lavazza team did have some problems. The captain was quite ill and could not fly, so the copilot, who did not have much experience, was flying. The autopilot did not work, and they had been bounced around severely going through the storms. They did not have a storm-scope and were not able to avoid as many of them as we did.

The next day when we went to the airport for our departure to Hong Kong, we saw the reason for the controller's concern and realized how dangerous our first approach had been. Towers and hills surround the field. Although these are shown on the approach plate, nothing drives the presence of obstructions home like the view of a strange airport with all of its pimples showing. It was not safe for him to vector us in as he had done.

We were one of the first to land in Guangzhou, and after going to the hotel, we had lunch with Marc and Steve and then decided to walk around the city. Our short walk turned into a long walk of probably 10 miles. We saw a lot of the city, including the shopping area and the harbor. We crossed a pedestrian bridge over a wide street and saw wall-to-wall bicycles as far as we could see in each direction. It felt much more alive and Western than Beijing, and more colorful. The city was quite busy and was probably a big tourist area. The weather was nice, and even warm.

Our hotel was almost luxurious and our room was beautiful. There was no room service, and we were told that in order to obtain drinks, we had to go to the service desk, which was located on each floor. The service desk, however, also did not have drinks and provided little service.

The official whom we had first met in Kunming and who sat at our table in Beijing was in Guangzhou as well, and he was waiting for us as we exited the elevator. He had brought us a book about China, which he autographed. Even though he said he had already eaten, he asked if he could take us to dinner. The organization had scheduled a dinner for us, so we declined. Jim also was concerned that it might require more toasting.

After dinner, there was a briefing on the procedure for flying into Hong Kong the next day, and we were advised that we would fly into Hong Kong in the afternoon, so would not have to go out to the airport until late morning or early afternoon.

Thursday, March 12, 1987

The phone in our room rang at approximately twenty minutes to 9:00. Plans had changed, and we were advised that we needed to be on the

The nose damage from the storm to Jim Knuppe's airplane.

bus at 9:00 a.m. to depart for the airport. Hong Kong was going to contact Guangzhou as soon as they were ready to accept airplanes, and so we had to be prepared to leave as soon as we were called.

Therefore, all of the competitors went to the airport early, even though we did not know what time we would be called or allowed to fly into Hong Kong. It takes less than an hour to fly from Guangzhou to Hong Kong, so we hoped that we could leave early and have the whole day in Hong Kong.

On arriving at the airport, we saw Jim Knuppe's 421C, *AAAAA-Rent-A-Space*. The paint on the nose was nicked, and there was a hole at the top of the nose that either had been pierced by a big hailstone or else hit by lightning. Jim thought the former, but it is difficult to see how a hailstone could do that much damage.

12

Guangzhou to Hong Kong

Thursday, March 12, 1987

We departed Guangzhou for Kai Tak Airport in Hong Kong. The twin-engine aircraft departed first, and they executed the IGS (Instrument Guidance System) for runway 13. This is a tricky approach, as it guides you to the top of a hill, not the runway.

If you fly the approach "down to minimums," you see a checkerboard panel on the hilltop. Then you turn a hard right and dive for the runway. You cannot drop below the published minimums or turn early because of all the tall buildings downtown. There usually is a crosswind that makes the landing even more difficult. In addition, the runway is relatively short, and if you come in too fast, there is a danger of going off the end and into the bay. Interesting place to land! (Kai Tak has since been replaced by a new, modern airport on an island to the southwest.)

There was a long delay before the single-engine aircraft were allowed to depart, so we spent most of the day waiting on the tarmac at Guangzhou. We had not eaten breakfast, since we had only twenty minutes to dress, pack, and get on the bus. It seemed that we were too often hungry on this trip.

Since we had cleared customs, we thought it would be highly unlikely that they would let us leave for lunch. However, the officials were accommodating, and they allowed us to leave on the bus, return to the hotel, have lunch, and then return to the airport without passing through customs again.

The single-engine aircraft finally departed for Hong Kong in late afternoon. We departed from runway 21, made a right ascending turn over the airport, and went directly to Shilong (LQ) NDB, where we turned right on A-461 en route to Hong Kong. The weather was beautiful most of the way, but became overcast as we approached the city.

Shortly after, we were turned over to the Hong Kong controller, and he vectored us directly to Cheung Chau (CH), and thereafter we were vectored for the ILS runway 31 approach. Although the twin-engine airplanes had been allowed to fly over the city to the famous checkerboard on the hill and land to the east, the single-engine airplanes were not allowed to fly over the city. This was interesting, since all other airplanes, including the large 747 commercial flights, were landing one way, to the east, and we were landing the other direction, to the west, on the one runway of Kai Tak Airport.

Shortly before descending into Hong Kong, we were in the clouds, and we flew IFR on the glideslope until we broke through about 500 feet above the runway.

This approach brought us in from the sea to the runway, and on this particular day, it was complicated by a 15-knot tailwind. To make matters worse, the controller kept us high until we were on the localizer inbound. We were coming in on the localizer "like a bat out of hell."

Since we were landing between commercial aircraft going the opposite direction from us, it was important that we keep our speed up as much as possible. Again, we shot the approach to minimums. What a thrill to break out at the decision height and see the city and surrounding hills. The weather was overcast, but the city appeared beautiful and modern.

13

Hong Kong

Thursday, March 12, 1987

Hong Kong became a colony of the British Empire at the end of the First Opium War in 1842 and expanded to the Kowloon Peninsula in 1860 after the Second Opium War. It was further extended when Britain obtained a ninety-nine-year lease of the New Territories in 1898.

Hong Kong is one of the world's leading international financial centers and hosts the largest concentration of ultra–high net worth individuals of any city in the world. It has the largest number of skyscrapers of any city in the world, and its residents have some of the highest life expectancies. The territory was returned to China in 1997 and is now officially the "Hong Kong Special Administrative Region of the People's Republic of China." We were there before the changeover, while it was still British.

On our first evening in Hong Kong, we attended a dinner and awards ceremony at the Hong Kong Foreign Correspondents Club, which is an interesting, exclusive, members-only club. Anne Speake, the president of International English Institute, one of our sponsors, and her daughter, Judy, were in Hong Kong to greet us, and they accompanied us to the event.

True to his word, David Beechcroft-Kay repaid the money that we had loaned him in Dhaka. We also met his lovely wife, Terry, who was to become a valued, longtime friend and great shopping guide.

David and Kevin's photojournalist was Bonnie Engel, an American and assistant chief editor of the magazine *Off Duty* in Hong Kong. She had lived there for many years, was a member of the Foreign Correspondents Club, and a respected videographer. She usually managed to do or say something to keep us laughing—some of which cannot be printed!

Friday, March 13, 1987

Alain from F Productions in Paris asked me if I would do an interview in French for French TV from a sampan in the Hong Kong harbor. I agreed, as long as someone would help me with the questions and answers if I stumbled, as it had been many, many years since I had taken a French course, and I felt quite rusty.

I took a cab to the embarkation point for the floating restaurants at Aberdeen in Hong Kong harbor with Reza, the race photographer; Maurice, the journalist from the *Bio-France Elevage* team; and La Girafe. The cab driver was confused. He was supposed to follow the F Productions video team. However, he lost them after approximately two blocks.

We returned to the hotel so that someone could explain to him in Chinese where we were supposed to go, but he still did not seem to know exactly where he was going and had to stop several times to ask directions. When we finally got to the meeting place, no one else was there. We assumed that they had given us up for lost and left without us.

While we were waiting, Reza made up a song for La Girafe and sang it to him to keep us entertained. He became La Girafe's best friend during the race.

The others had not left us. Their taxi driver also had been lost and took them to another point on the harbor. They managed to hire a sampan, so they soon pulled up to the dock where we were waiting, picked us up, and then returned to meet the TV crew on a second sampan. We motored around Aberdeen Harbour for approximately four hours doing the interview.

The interviewer asked me about our airplane, how I enjoyed flying the race with my husband, about being the first US woman and first female private pilot to land in China, and about La Girafe and the hospital.

With photographer Reza and La Girafe waiting at the harbor.

I explained that Jim and I were flying this race to raise money for a children's hospital in our home city, Fresno, California, and that the residents of the city were able to pledge money for each leg of the race that we completed. I explained that the giraffe was the mascot of the hospital, and he had traveled with us from Fresno to Paris to Beijing to Hong Kong and would be with us for the remainder of the race.

On several occasions, my answer was interrupted by a long, loud blast from the horn of a passing boat, and we would have to do another take, but this worked out well, as it gave me a chance to improve my grammar. I thought that the interview went well and was told that it was subsequently broadcast in France.

I thought that I had seen every type of bathroom until we docked. Hong Kong is a beautiful city and has many nice bathrooms, but on the day that I did the interview, we had cruised around the harbor for quite a while. When we disembarked, it was important for me to find a bathroom immediately, and I asked the elderly lady who was helping us disembark if there was a hotel or office building or anything nearby with facilities that I could use.

She shook her head no, but motioned to a door nearby that looked as though it was connected to nothing. It simply looked like a door and a doorframe on the edge of the dock. She indicated that I was to go through it, but since it was on the edge of the dock, I wondered if it was not simply an invitation to step into the harbor.

When I opened the door, I saw that there was a "room," no bigger than the width of the door, perhaps three feet by three feet max. This room had no floor and no ceiling, but there was one narrow board on each side where the floor ordinarily would be. It was not possible to enter and then turn around, since there was no floor, so I gingerly backed in, one foot on each board at the edge of the "room," and looked down. There was the harbor. Hoping that there were no scuba divers below, I added to the harbor fluid. It was a most unusual sensation.

Jim spent the day at the airport tending to the airplane and getting it refueled. It also got its 100-hour maintenance.

That evening, dinner was on Lamma Island. We traveled by junk with a well-stocked bar on board. First of all, we were taken on a sightseeing tour around the island and Victoria Harbour, then to the far side of the island and away from land. We saw the area where we had boarded the sampans that morning, which was brightly lit and beautiful at night. We also passed some other islands and saw the area called the New Territories.

The boat ride was approximately one hour long, and it was beautiful to ride off into the setting sun with Hong Kong in the background. Unfortunately, Jim did not return from the airport in time to go, so Anne Speake and her daughter, Judy, went with me and a majority of the other competitors and technical people.

Lamma Island was not fancy, but the food was delicious, and we ate in an open-air restaurant overlooking the water. Allen and his friend, Annette, who had joined us in Beijing and followed us to Hong Kong, were sitting with their backs to the water, and every time we collected too many shrimp shells, bones, or other residue on our plates, we would pass them over to Allen and he would toss them over his shoulder into the water. It was wonderful to be warm after the cold, cold weather of Beijing. I felt as though I was finally thawing out.

Saturday, March 14, 1987

Jeannie Lee, a friend of Helen and Stan's, who were former neighbors of mine in Fresno, called me. Stan now lived primarily in Hong Kong, but he and Helen also had a home in Idaho. Helen had told Jeannie about the race and that I would be in Hong Kong. She offered to take me shopping, and of course I accepted, since Helen had told me that Jeannie knew all the good places to shop.

At breakfast, Anne's daughter, Judy, was not feeling well, and her right side in particular hurt her. Anne was concerned that it might be her appendix, as she had never had it removed. I asked Bernard if there was a doctor, and he directed me to Michel, the pilot of *Le Havre–Normandie*, who said that her temperature should be taken. I told him I would try to find a thermometer, and he said that he would try as well.

We took Anne and Judy to our room, and I went to the desk to find a thermometer. The concierge said that he would have one delivered to our room. I returned to our room where Anne and Judy were waiting and began to sort laundry and dry cleaning, as it was necessary to have the laundry done that day before we moved on. I called housekeeping to pick up the laundry, which I was sorting in the hallway between the front door and the bedroom, when Jean Le Ber and Jean-Michel came by to see what we were doing and have a glass of champagne with Jim.

Next, Dr. Michel came back to check Judy, as he now had a thermometer. He was examining Judy on the bed. Jean and Jean-Michel were talking to Jim and Anne and drinking champagne. I was sorting laundry in the middle of the hall, and someone came to deliver another thermometer. We kept it, as we thought that Judy might need one later, but this necessitated me signing several documents indicating that it had been received and promising that it would be returned.

Jeannie Lee then arrived to take me shopping. Michel was telling Judy that she should get undressed so that he could examine her better. Housekeeping came to pick up the laundry, which was not yet sorted but strewn all over the floor. With a room full of people, Judy was not about to get undressed for some strange doctor who spoke French. He wanted to insert the thermometer in one end, and she wanted it in the other. The translation was quite clear!

The laundry was finally disposed of, the fellow with the second thermometer left, and the phone rang. It was Stan to give me the name of a jeweler friend. Michel finished his examination and prescribed some medication for Judy. He said she should watch her temperature closely, and if it became elevated, she would need further examination to determine whether or not it was due to her appendix.

Since we had finished the champagne, everyone else finally left, and Jeannie and I went shopping. Judy was fine for the rest of the trip, but Dr. Michel was attentive. We thought that he may have given her special attention as she is attractive, though, in reality, he was probably just being a good and thorough doctor.

Jeannie took me to Stanley Market. Our hotel was in Kowloon on the other side of Hong Kong Harbour, so we took a taxi on the ferry across to Hong Kong Island and then for about another hour's drive after that. Stanley Market is a large area of small shops, interspersed with restaurants.

After stopping in the first three shops, I had purchased so much that I needed to purchase a suitcase. I found an expandable one that began about eighteen inches high, but then unzipped in a circular motion and grew until it was almost five feet tall. Fortunately, it had a stiff bottom and was on wheels.

As the day progressed, I filled up the suitcase entirely, to its full height, primarily with silk dresses, blouses, robes, and such as gifts for family and friends. The prices were so incredibly low that I could not pass up the bargains.

Jeannie and I paused once in our (or rather my) shopping spree to have lunch. The restaurant appeared to be a typical neighborhood restaurant and not at all similar to those in the hotel or where we had previously eaten, and I ate with some trepidation. However, I had no problems. If I had, I probably would not have noticed, as I was too preoccupied with the shopping. The cab dropped Jeannie off at or near where she lives and took me back to the Holiday Inn Golden Mile, where we were staying.

I went to the concierge to inquire about shipping my purchases home, as it was way too much to carry in our airplane. I was told that I would need to obtain a license, as I was shipping in commercial quantities. I did not think I was buying that much, but I did buy gifts for a lot of people.

Obviously, I would not have time to obtain a license, so I spoke to David, the Cathay Pacific captain who frequently flew the Hong Kong–San Francisco route. He agreed to bring my purchases with him each time he flew to San Francisco over the next months. He joked that it was probably one of the few places where they would not question him for carrying a suitcase full of women's clothes.

I had contacted Stan, my old friend. He and his wife, Helen, used to be my neighbors in Fresno, and he had taught me about Chinese (Cantonese) cooking, daily use of a wok, and how to count to ten in Cantonese. Stan is an artist and was teaching painting at Fresno State, but his family wanted him to return to Hong Kong to participate in the family business. In addition to his home in Hong Kong, he and Helen built a home in Idaho where Helen lived during the school year with their son. Stan traveled back and forth.

Stan said that even though he would be busy that day, he would like to come by to see me and meet Jim that evening. We had a dinner to attend, but agreed to meet him afterward, at approximately 9:00 p.m. at the hotel bar. He arrived, and we had a couple of drinks together and reminisced until fairly late.

I told him about my problem with the license to ship my purchases home, and he offered to store them at his office so that David could pick up some each time he flew to San Francisco. Stan agreed to have his chauffeur come to our hotel the next morning to pick up the suitcase that I had filled with my purchases. What a relief it was to have that problem resolved.

That night, the official dinner at the hotel was hosted by Martell Cognac. We were each given a bottle of Martell brandy with a label commemorating the race. We were also given a small plate with the emblem of the race imprinted on it. The guests of honor were the French consul, Cultural Attaché, and local authorities.

Since we would be flying across the South China Sea to Manila the next day, the longest overwater flight of the trip, Bernard asked Jim if we had a hammer.

"A hammer?" Jim asked. "Why would we need to have a hammer?"

Bernard explained that an airplane had gone into the ocean near New-foundland some years ago, and the pilots would have been rescued except that because of the pressure of the water against the airplane doors, they could not open them.

"You need a hammer," Bernard reiterated. "Then if you go into the sea, you can break through the front window and escape."

Jim found a store and bought a hammer.

14

Hong Kong to Singapore

Sunday, March 15, 1987

Winged Quest departed Hong Kong for Singapore. Two fuel stops were required en route, one in Manila and the other in Kota Kinabalu, Malaysia, on the island of Borneo. The airplanes that were going to Singapore via Manila were allowed to depart first, and we were lucky enough to be the first aircraft to depart.

The Hong Kong airport and officials were perhaps the most unfriendly of the whole air race. In fact, they were downright rude. Just getting to our aircraft was a problem that morning. It was obvious that Hong Kong did not want the race to pass through its airport at all. Many little obstructions were placed in the way of an orderly arrival and departure. All of the crews, including the Cathay Pacific crew flying *Spirit of Hong Kong* (David, Kevin, and Bonnie), were required to depart as though we were airline passengers.

Not only were we required to stand in line while they issued us commercial boarding passes, but we all were required to pay an exorbitant fee as a departure tax for one passenger, presumably for the photojournalist, notwithstanding our contention that he was part of the crew. The final straw was that we had to file through the passenger terminal, go through a security check with electronic scanners, and have our luggage inspected. Would we seriously consider blowing up our own airplanes?

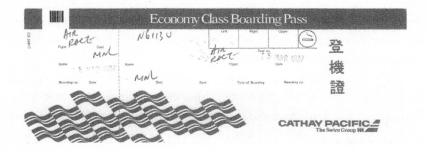

Boarding pass issued in Hong Kong to allow
us to board our own airplane.

We received boarding passes as though we were boarding a 747 for the United States before being allowed onto the tarmac to go to our airplanes. Absurd! We do not know whether they thought that we were going to bomb our own airplanes, or whether they simply wished to hassle us. We suspected the latter. The competitors agreed that no other place, not any city or any government, was as rude to us as in Hong Kong.

When we arrived at our airplane, we already knew that Haeco (Hong Kong Aircraft Engineering Co., Ltd.) had removed everything we had left in the aircraft—survival gear, handheld transceiver, and other gear—and stored them in their office. This was done for so-called security reasons and without our permission, and they even removed our HF radio and Sat Nav.

They brought everything back to the airplane and supposedly reinstalled everything that they had uninstalled. What we did not know is that they had disconnected our Sat Nav. It was not until we were lined up ready to depart and turned on our Sat Nav that we discovered that they had not reconnected it. Even though we then reconnected it, it would not work.

When we taxied out for takeoff that morning, we expected to use the Sat Nav to establish our position for the required position reports when we were over the South China Sea. The Sat Nav just simply would not operate. In fact, it never worked again during the entire trip. We had a number of qualified folks look at it, but no one could get it to operate again. There was nothing we could do about it. We simply had to establish our position by reference to our watch and compass when we were out of range of the VORs. We never had to do this while flying in the States, but it seemed that we were doing it a lot on this trip.

Hong Kong control was also not cooperative. They directed us to a holding point that was not marked, either on the airport chart or on the airport itself, and then seemed surprised that we taxied past it. They made us hold for approximately twenty minutes while they allowed airliners to depart, even though we easily could have safely departed between them, and certainly would have been allowed to in Los Angeles or San Francisco.

Although we loved our time in Hong Kong, we were both relieved to leave this inhospitable airport.

We finally departed Hong Kong and flew across the South China Sea toward the Philippine Islands.[7] Our overwater reports were passed along by airliners and, as always, they were a great help. The weather was good. There is never much to say about an overwater flight that goes smoothly other than, "Boy, there is a lot of water out there!"

The airplane performed perfectly, and our navigation was excellent. We arrived at the reporting points and San Fernando when we should have. The Philippine Islands were beautiful. The first island that we flew over, Luzon, was green. The sun was shining brightly, and it was lovely. What a perfect day for a flight. At one point, there were many small islands around the larger one, and it appeared that we were flying over a topographical map.

We landed in Manila at about 13:17. Manila looked like a beautiful city, and we wished that we could see more of it. The island, at that point, is so narrow that from the air one can see the water on both sides. Manila is built in the narrowest part of the island, and there is a lot of water in the city itself. The airport is somewhat outside of the city, so we could not see much of it from the ground.

---

7. We had departed on runway 13, intercepted the 132-degree radial from the Cheung Chau (CH) VOR, which established us on A-461. The mandatory overwater reporting points were D100 (which one could establish from CH, believe it or not), AKHRO, and VELVO. We reached land at San Fernando (SAN), from which we proceeded to Cabanatuan (CAB), and then direct to Manila, The Philippines.

Coming in to land in Manila.

Our reception at Manila was fantastic. There were many townspeople, as well as TV and newspaper reporters and the usual array of officials. Reporters and photographers surrounded us. They were excited when we landed, as we were the first race airplane to land in Manila, and they thought that we were winning the race.

When, in response to a reporter's question, Jim told him that we were not leading the race, he responded, "Well, at least you won the race to Manila!" Our picture was taken, we were interviewed, and we appeared on the front page of the Manila paper.

As was typical wherever we landed, many military personnel would mill around the aircraft. They often collected fees of one sort or another. In Manila, a middle-aged military type dressed in a splendid white uniform was introduced to us, and we were told that he was there to collect the landing fee. The landing fee was a modest $20. Jim did not have $20 but only a $50 bill, which he handed to the spiffily-dressed military type. He snatched the bill from Jim and deposited it in his pocket. He then turned on his heels and walked off. Needless to say, we never saw our change.

Nevertheless, after a friendly and expeditious stop, we were refueled and on our way again. The refueling and processing was so quick, and the people were so friendly, that we felt welcome and hoped to return. This was reinforced as we flew over the rest of the beautiful Philippine Islands.

We departed Manila at 14:10 for Kota Kinabalu, our next refueling stop.[8] On leaving Manila, we were reminded again of World War II history. We saw the island of Corregidor from which Gen. Douglas MacArthur escaped in a PT boat. We next saw the Bataan Peninsula, where American and Philippine soldiers were forced to walk to an internment camp. This is commonly referred to as the Bataan Death March, since so many died from mistreatment, dehydration, and starvation.

After that, we flew over more water to another island. It was somewhat more green and lush, and the deep forest made a beautiful contrast to the golden sands of the beaches and the deep blue of the sea. On the north side of the first island, we occasionally saw white foam as the waves bubbled around the shore. In other places, the water was still, and there was a sense of isolation and quiet. So many places beckoned us to stop and stay awhile.

We flew over some of the most beautiful islands in the world. At least from the air they appeared that way. The islands included Mindoro and Palawan, which is almost three hundred nautical miles long. What a sight! What an experience! The island was green and the water was so blue. The sky was clear. The visibility was unlimited. We were snapping pictures as fast as possible. Perhaps our luck had changed. Perhaps the bad weather was behind us.

As we flew over Palawan Island, we realized that it was much larger than the island on which Manila is located. This island also had roads, cities, and obviously people. The weather was beautiful and clear, and we were entranced by the beauty of the island and sea below.

At one point, we saw what appeared to be an old airfield that we assumed was in use during World War II. It was near the water, and there did not seem to be any city nearby. If it had been farther inland, the jungle would have long since claimed it.

---

8. The route was W-2 to the Kota Kinabalu FIR, then W-20 to Kota Kinabalu.

Greetings at the airport in Kota Kinabalu, Borneo.

As we left the Philippine Islands, we headed toward our next stop, Kota Kinabalu, Borneo. As we neared Kota Kinabalu, we passed by Mount Kinabalu, a magnificent mountain located on the northwest part of Borneo and rising some 13,435 feet out of the jungle and over the island floor, which was only slightly above sea level. Patches of snow covered its shoulders—that part above the tree line. The top of the mountain was shrouded in clouds, and we could only imagine its majesty. Quite a view in a tropical setting.

We landed at Kota Kinabalu at 17:30, and our stop was a repeat of the stop in Manila. Many townspeople had come to see us, and we thought that probably it was everyone in the town. The media wanted their interviews, and the officials were friendly and helpful. The processing was quick, and they provided us with beverages.

One cameraman had been a friend and colleague of Reza's and knew him from the Philippines when they were both filming the overthrow of the Marcos regime and rise to power of Corazon Aquino. He told us that Reza had nearly been killed and had been hit in the head and wounded when someone threw a rock. He said that Reza was well known and respected in the world of international photography.

 We were promptly and courteously processed. We paid the fees and for the fuel and departed at 18:10 for the night flight to Singapore. We left Kota Kinabalu, again wishing that we could stay longer in this place and explore it further.

Because of severe thunderstorms over Borneo, we headed slightly more out to sea than our course directed. We watched with fascination as the lightning seemed to light up the clouds from the inside, much like a group of synchronized fireflies trapped in a bottle.

Our path was smooth, and we soon skirted around the storm and headed toward the distant sunset. The sun seemed to perch on a shelf of clouds just above the water, and then it slowly slipped behind them into the sea, leaving only the gold-rimmed clouds, which gradually turned dark.

We flew just off the west coast of Borneo, by Brunei (where the controller was courteous), taking essentially G-580 to Kucing (VKG), which is located on the southwest tip of the island, then G-580 direct to Singapore. The flight took about four and one-half hours. We received vectors to Seletar Airport, which does not have an instrument approach.

We landed at Singapore–Seletar airport and were greeted by a young girl, Miss Singapore, who pinned an orchid on my vest. As we had come to expect, we also were met by the usual photographers (French and local) and the organization personnel. We were proud to have flown over such a forbidding part of the world in a single-engine aircraft that was not equipped with any special navigation aids. We still can hardly believe that we did it without a problem.

The processing through customs did not take long, and we were soon on our way to the Holiday Inn Parkview, a luxurious new hotel.

15

Singapore

Sunday, March 15, 1987

Singapore existed as a trading settlement as early as the fourteenth century. In 1819, Sir Thomas Stamford Raffles negotiated a treaty whereby the British were allowed to locate a trading port on the island, leading to the establishment of the British colony of Singapore.

During World War II, Singapore was conquered and occupied by the Japanese. When the war ended, it reverted to British control with increasing levels of self-government being granted, culminating in Singapore's merger with the Federation of Malaya to form Malaysia in 1963. Disputes resulted in Singapore's expulsion from Malaysia, and it became an independent republic in 1965.

Singapore, situated at the tip of the Malay Peninsula, is a city-state. It has a land area of only 238.5 square miles, with a population of more than 2.5 million. It has a thriving economy, being astride one of the world's busiest trade routes, the Strait of Malacca, through which passes most of the oil bound to Japan from the Middle East and the goods bound for Europe from Japan, Taiwan, China, and South Korea.

Usually four hundred ships are anchored in the harbor at Singapore at any one time. It has been estimated that a ship arrives every ten minutes. The name Singapore comes from the "Singa Pura," meaning Lion City.

Singapore is a shopper's dream. Shoppers often say that it is less expensive than Hong Kong.

Monday, March 16, 1987

I went shopping in the morning and Jim went to the pool. I intended to return to the hotel by 3:00 p.m. for the press conference. However, in Singapore, shopping is much more time-consuming than in Hong Kong. In Hong Kong, one would simply ask for a quantity discount and the price would be reduced about ten or twenty percent from the already low price. In Singapore, the prices were almost as high as in the States, so it was necessary (and expected) to bargain over each item.

My main purchases in Singapore were watches for our sons, daughters, daughter-in-law, and mother. This entailed a great deal of negotiation. The first day, I negotiated for a long time regarding watches for our two sons. I was told that I would probably get the watches for forty-two percent off the regular price, and finally got to the point where I felt that I was getting a good bargain, but told the salesman that I would come back the next day, as I had to buy watches for our daughters as well. In addition, our negotiations broke down somewhat, as I wished to charge the watches on a credit card. If I paid cash, I would get a larger discount.

Jim had gone to the Raffles Hotel to sip a Singapore Sling in the Long Bar. Supposedly the drink was invented at Raffles in 1915 and consists of a refreshing mixture of gin, cherry brandy, lime juice, Cointreau or Benedictine, bitters, and soda.

Jean Le Ber and Jean-Michel joined Jim in partaking of the famous Singapore Sling, and the three of them then visited the hotel's small museum. Memorabilia of every sort was for sale. Among the items for sale was a pith helmet. Jim pronounced the word *pith* for Jean and Jean-Michel, and they promptly pronounced it a "piss" helmet. This brought a number of chuckles from the English-speaking people who overheard their conversation.

In the adjoining room to the Long Bar—and this was before noon—American tourists were already being introduced to local "culture," which consisted of a combination of hula dances and Asian music.

Raffles no longer is the home of famous writers. The likes of Somerset

Maugham do not stalk the bars and public areas looking for a situation to include in a novel. Nevertheless, Jim enjoyed every minute of his visit. The hotel had just celebrated its hundredth birthday in 1986. The stories the old place could tell!

In the afternoon, Jim joined a number of the French participants in the garden at Raffles, where the French television crew was shooting some scenes to transmit to Paris. Everyone was seated around tables sipping Singapore Slings during the filming.

On-camera interviews were part of the program. Since Jim does not speak French, they did not ask him anything on camera, but he did serve as part of the background. However, David Beechcroft-Kay knew one French expression, *"Mon petit chou, voulez-vous promenade avec moi ce soir?"* On camera, he directed his comment to Claudine Sobol-Oosterlinck of the Novasam team, seated next to him.

She blushed and everyone laughed, including the cameraman. A loose translation would be, "My little cabbage, would you like to walk with me this evening?" Apparently, the word *cabbage* is a word of endearment in France. Since this exchange was to be broadcast over French television that day, Claudine called her husband in Paris to warn him of the broadcast and to explain that it was totally innocent.

For the remainder of the race, Claudine was known as *petit chou*. Even over our common radio frequency, one could often hear her called by that name.

That evening, we went to the awards ceremony at the offices of the Alliance Française. There was a huge poster with the blue, white, and red of the French flag on one end, and the red with gold stars representing the Chinese flag on the other end, and the middle was a beautiful sky with scattered clouds and about a dozen airplanes of various types. The top of the poster read "Rallye Paris-Pekin 1987," and on the bottom of the poster were Chinese characters, evidently saying the same.

It was quite striking and was set at the edge of a lawn framed by the green shrubbery and trees. We took pictures of most of the crews against this backdrop. The buffet dinner was more meager than some and more like hors d'oeuvres, but there was plenty of wine, and everyone was in a party mood.

Race director Bernard Lamy (seated) with his family
(from left), son Didier, wife Maryse, daughter Patricia,
and son Bruno in front of the race poster at the Alliance
Française office during the reception in Singapore.

The building, which was open to the yard, had a piano, and soon Gaston and Jean-Pierre Malignon began a boogie duet. Patricia began dancing first with her brother Didier and then with her father, Bernard. Others joined in, either dancing or keeping time with the music. Miss Singapore was at this reception and accompanied us again the next evening as we took a boat tour around the harbor.

Since our early dinner this evening had been rather light, we went back to the hotel and then decided to go to the top of the Mandarin Hotel for a view of Singapore and a more formal dinner. Jean, Jean-Michel, Gilles, Anne, and her daughter, Judy, all went with us. We had a beautiful dinner high above Singapore, watching the lights of the city.

Tuesday, March 17, 1987

After breakfast, I went back to the watch shop and negotiated again for the watches. This time, I had some cash, so I managed to negotiate a cash price, but then, since I did not have enough cash, I put half of the purchases on a credit card and only paid half in cash. The price held, however, and I bought the watches for approximately a third of the original price. I had been told that both in Hong Kong and in Singapore, it is expected that the quoted prices are negotiable.

I did more shopping and then returned to the hotel. It was only after I arrived at the hotel and showed Jim my watch purchases that he said, "Didn't you get a watch for yourself?" I had totally forgotten, and now there was no more time.

We went to the airport as we were scheduled to fly our airplane, along with the camera crew that would be flying in the Chronopost airplane. They would take pictures of us in flight, and also perhaps send one of the camera crew with us on our airplane so that they could get some shots of us in the airplane, since Allen was not taking videos. When we arrived at the airport, we were not able to go with the first group, as we needed to refuel.

Seletar Airport is on the airbase for the Singapore Air Force. Many of the young pilots or workers were curious and came to talk to us and see our airplane, and several of them wanted to be photographed with us. Of course, as usual, we agreed and had a great photo session.

It was hot, and we ended up spending a long period of time getting refueled. Some of the airplanes had major problems, such as Jim Knuppe's 421C, *AAAAA-Rent-A-Space.* They practically had to rebuild one of its engines. One of the Italian airplanes also had major problems, and David's 335, *Spirit of Hong Kong*, had problems as well. The workers at the Seletar FBO seemed to be very good and knew what they were doing, and they were kept busy with our group.

The afternoon wore on, and the weather became menacing. Soon it appeared that we could no longer take photographs because the clouds were too dense, so we returned to the hotel.

Dinner that night was on a junk cruising around the harbor. As we boarded the bus, it began raining hard. We were afraid that we would be soaked, but shortly after we got to the boat, the rain stopped, and it was a lovely evening.

In Singapore, the Kouros Yves Saint-Laurent team delivered flowers to our room and also gave me a pendant with Opium perfume inside. They gave ties and other gifts to the men as well. We wondered where they had kept all of the gifts, as their airplane would have been weighted down, but then realized that they probably had them shipped to Singapore.

16

Singapore to Bombay

Wednesday, March 18, 1987

This was the day we were to leave for Bombay, and everyone hoped to leave early as we had a long flight ahead of us. However, the first airplanes could not leave until after 15:00, since there were some officials who wished to wave off the airplanes, and they would not be arriving until that time, at least.

We had drawn a high number, so would not be leaving until close to 17:00. This did not make us terribly happy as, again, we would be flying all night. Obviously, the officials thought that it was more important to be seen with us at their convenience than for us to fly safely during the daylight. We wished they would have given more thought to us.

We finally departed Seletar Airport in Singapore at 16:15 for the long flight to Bombay, India.[9] Our flight plan called for a four-and-one-half-hour flight to Bangkok, our first fuel stop. The route took us due north over the Malay Peninsula.

We, being one of the last airplanes to depart, took off into menacing weather conditions. It was cloudy with thunderstorms to the north and

---

9. We departed Seletar, climbed to 8,000 feet, flying direct to Mersing (VMR), B-469 to Kota Bharu (VKB), B-69 to REGOS, then A-64/B-69 direct to Bangkok (BKK).

west, but, fortunately, the main body of the storms was to the west of our track. We could see the flashes of lightning off in the distance, but we soared undisturbed en route to our destination.

After a bit, we could see more of the terrain, and it was beautiful. The Malay Peninsula was awash in water, with rivers bounding down to the sea from the high ground. The jungle opened to allow this much-needed drainage. Some of the rivers were dammed, storing water for irrigation and energy purposes. In other places, there were medium-sized mountains. The landscape was stunning. We agreed that this would be a place to which we would love to return and explore.

Jim Knuppe in *AAAAA-Rent-A-Space* had decided to fly directly to Sri Lanka across the Indian Ocean. On landing in Colombo, he had barely twenty minutes of fuel remaining. To his surprise, he found that there was no 100-octane aviation fuel available in Colombo. That was something that should have been checked, but, like we probably would have done, he assumed that airports have fuel. He was forced to take a local controller with him and fly to another nearby airport for fuel. Too close for comfort!

At Kota Bharu, we departed the peninsula for the last time for the 500-nautical-mile flight over the Gulf of Thailand and then on to Bangkok.

Dusk was beginning to turn to dark shortly after we left the coast, but approximately halfway across the bay, with no land in sight, we saw the most striking sunset of the trip. The clouds streaked across the western sky, with one stack of particularly dense clouds arising from the edge of the sea connecting to the higher level of clouds. This lower area was a brilliant gold, which almost seemed to shimmer. It was reflected off our left wing, which looked as though it was gold-plated.

Above this level of clouds, the sky was a translucent green-blue and higher, farther to the east, was a thin layer of clouds that looked like angel hair, alternating between mauve and deep blue gray, depending on the clouds' relationship to the sunset.

The word *breathtaking* hardly does justice to the sky that evening. We were enthralled by the beauty of it all. The entire panorama was reflected in the sea, and with our gold wings, we truly felt a part of the spectacle.

Our engine hummed along beautifully, and each of us was silent, not

A breathtaking sunset bathed our wings in gold
between Singapore and Bangkok.

wishing to speak or even breathe, savoring this moment of natural per-
fection. As the sun descended, the colors changed and dulled, and as the
last rays slipped beyond the edge of the earth, we could see hundreds of
tiny lights below, either from ships or oil rigs in the bay and then, soon, the
lights of Bangkok.

The weather was good in Bangkok when we landed at 20:50. On landing, I saw to the refueling while Jim went to the terminal to take care of
the paperwork and pay the landing fees and other charges. The refueling
did not take long, once I could find someone who understood what we
wanted, and they brought the fuel truck to our area. Several airplanes
arrived after us, and they also were refueled fairly quickly.

The paperwork, however, was another story. For Jim, the fun was just
beginning. Evidently, the speed of the processing depended upon which
customs agent one had. Bernard Lamy and the technical team had the
same customs agent that Jim had. It took Jim three hours and forty minutes to process, and Bernard even longer.

On arriving at the terminal, Jim was taken to the offices of Thai Airways International Limited. It was explained that Thai Airways would act as our agent, which would greatly speed up the processing. To his surprise, two other crews were in the office. They were Chuck Rosenquist's crew, Jeff Bennett and Tim Knatchbull, and the French crew of the organization's King Air 200.

Jim had also seen the TDK crew moving briskly through the terminal. What was so surprising was that all three of these aircraft had departed Singapore long before we had. We all soon learned that Thai bureaucracy could match the Egyptians for inefficiency.

Some of the competitors who arrived after us took substantially less time, and most of them were gone by the time Jim reappeared outside at our airplane. The Cathay Pacific team had an agent in Bangkok, and one of the Cathay pilots who had originally been invited by David to fly the race with him was there with all of the paperwork prepared in advance for David's signature. Therefore, David only needed to refuel, and the 335 was off in twenty minutes. It really helps to be a professional pilot who has flown to these places previously and knows people. We were not so lucky.

Bangkok, Thailand, had the most well-guarded *toilette*. From the tarmac, it was necessary to convince the guard that there was a legitimate purpose for me to go into the terminal and upstairs. This guard called the guards over from the gate, and they had a conference regarding my request, but it was finally granted.

I walked up a winding incline, and at the top there were two more guards, and beyond them, a security area with the familiar walk-through and parcel X-ray. A door led into the waiting room, which was full of people, but I could not go straight through. It was necessary to again explain my purpose to the guards, who then allowed me into the X-ray area, and when I was processed through, I again had to go to the guards who let me through the main door.

There was another guard at the hallway, but luckily a flight attendant from Thai Airlines asked if she could help, and she escorted me through to the restroom. We were checked another time or two, but with her assistance, it took less time.

Returning to the airplane required the same process, in reverse, and the guards who had seen me ten minutes before again asked all of the same questions, even though they obviously recognized me and knew about the race and participants. The only people using that particular entrance would have been airline pilots or, perhaps, airport workers.

At one point, I thought that Jim must have been kidnapped, so I persuaded the fellow who had been helping me with the fuel that I needed to go and look for him. He took me past the first couple of security stations and then found a young lady from Thai Airlines who spoke English and who helped me get through the terminal and find Jim.

He was still running from place to place, getting signatures, but said that he was nearly finished. Therefore, I simply changed some money so Jim could pay the fees, got some sodas, and went back to the airplane to wait.

After what seemed an eternity, Jim paid the fees, and we were able to depart. The fees included charges for normal ground handling, landing fees, navigation fees, transport, and CIQ (whatever that meant, we did not know, but we paid it). The total frustrating process had taken over three and one-half hours. We finally departed at 00:30.

We filed and flew A-1 to Rangoon (HGU) and A-1 across the Bay of Bengal to Calcutta, India, our next refueling stop. Our flight level was 10,000 feet. The total distance was 871 nautical miles, but it took a disappointing five hours and fifteen minutes because of a strong headwind. It crossed our minds that whatever direction we flew, the winds knew and challenged us.

That part of the flight between Rangoon and Calcutta was expected to be routine because of the help of the Sittwe VOR (AKB) and several NDBs. But, as we often found in our flights in this exotic part of the world, one's expectations and reality are two quite different things.

Sittwe was inoperative, and none of the Burmese NDBs were functioning. We essentially flew the entire route by reference only to our watch and the compass. That was becoming common for us. It was obvious that the headwind was a lightly quartering wind (from the northwest), which was blowing us to the east. However, we could not tell exactly how far east.

We knew that it was some distance when we began to receive the

Chittagong VOR (CCTG). Jim immediately established a wind correction angle to the northwest, and, in short order, we began to receive the Calcutta VOR (CEA). The weather was good, so although we shot the ILS, it was essentially VFR.

In Calcutta, we reversed the process. Jim stayed with the airplane to see to the refueling, and I went to the terminal to complete the forms and pay the landing fees and other charges. The refueling was swift and courteous. The tanks required 385 liters (3.6 liters to a US gallon) to be topped. The gas cost $287.

First of all, I had to go into one office to give them our general declaration forms and sign some other papers. The gentlemen there were not terribly slow, but also were in no particular hurry. Extra personnel were standing around to answer every demand of the more senior personnel, and a "mess boy" delivered hot tea to each desk.

I was informed that the landing fee would have to be paid in local currency, so I would be escorted to the local bank. This involved hopping into an open military jeep-like vehicle with not only the driver but two military men armed with large automatic rifles. There was another gun, a machine gun, mounted on the back of the jeep. We drove fast through the dark, dodging around sacred cows, which were roaming free. I wondered if I would ever make it back to the terminal.

We drove to a small building that was a bank of sorts. Actually, it was simply a drive-by hole-in-the-wall with a barred window such as a teller in the bank would have. I easily changed the money. As usual, there were papers to be filled out and documents to sign, but again, this was not a lengthy process. I returned to the heavily armed jeep, which was waiting to escort me back to the terminal through the cows in the middle of the night. It seemed surreal.

When we arrived at the first office, I paid the landing fees in the local currency. I then filled out a flight plan and gave it to the gentleman expecting, of course, to leave. He advised me, however, that I must get our flight plan stamped by the weatherman in the Met office. This was directly down the hall, and as I got up to leave, Jim, who had finished refueling the airplane, entered. It had been about an hour, and he came to check on my progress. I told him about my adventurous trip to the bank.

We both went to the Met office, and when we arrived, there were a couple of other race people there, including Didier Lamy, who flew the Arc en Ciel organization's King Air and was also waiting for a briefing.

I sat down in front of the weatherman and requested that he stamp our fight plan. He said that he was much too busy to handle the matter and advised us that he would have to obtain a written weather report, which would take at least half an hour. He was drawing isometric lines on a chart by hand.

I told the weatherman that we could not wait that long, that we knew that the weather was clear from Calcutta to Bombay, we had a storm-scope, and that if he made us wait for half an hour, then he was going to cause us to lose the race.

Of course, we were not in any position to win the race, but it seemed a good argument to me at the time. He did not seem at all impressed and said that these were the rules.

I am usually fairly patient, easy going, and do not have a temper, but perhaps because of the delay in departing Singapore, the long stop in Bangkok, and because it was the middle of the night and I was tired, I became agitated.

I still kept my voice calm, but I again explained in a slightly louder voice to this person scribbling on a piece of paper that we were participants in an international air race and that our prompt departure was important to our success in the race.

The weatherman was not moved and stood his ground. He said that he did not give briefings of this type verbally. Instead, it was necessary to receive the briefing in a written format. The French were more stoic. They did not say much because they realized that to say too much might delay the process even more. I was not that perceptive.

Jim had wandered over to the side wall where the weather reports were hanging, and I asked him, "Jim, what is the weather like between here and Bombay from the charts?"

Jim said, "Clear," and I turned back to the weatherman and said, "Well, now I have my weather report. Please stamp my flight plan so that we can go."

He explained to me again that he would not do so until he had a written weather report to give me, that it was being typed, and that he would not stamp my flight plan until it was prepared.

While the impasse stalled our departure, two tall, good-looking gentlemen in white uniforms beautifully trimmed in gold (obviously airline captains) walked in. I thought perhaps they were British, so I explained to them in my best English my frustration with the process. They simply stared at me blankly with an amazed look on their faces, and I then turned back to berate the weatherman again.

Didier, Jim, and the other race people tried to calm me down, telling me that I would probably make things worse, so I decided that retreat was probably a better option. I asked my guide to show me where the *toilette* was. He put his large automatic rifle over his shoulder and motioned that he would escort me.

After my argument with the weatherman and after telling the amazed white-uniformed pilots what I thought of Indian bureaucracy, I left the Met office for the *toilette*, well-armed escort in tow. He took me down a long, dark hallway and finally to a room with no door. It crossed my mind that I was spending way too much time in dark places with heavily armed men.

The room was extremely dirty, obviously coed, but fortunately it did have a stall with a door. My well-armed escort stood guard while I went into the stall with the door to find, again, the now-familiar hole in the floor. I knew now to bring Kleenex and was prepared, but the guard, not knowing that, soon reached his hand under the door with toilet paper. That was a new experience for me.

I now had a unique experience and a few uninterrupted minutes to cool down, so I went back to the Met office, sat down, and silently glared at the weatherman. Finally, the Met official came up with the written report (which had suddenly materialized, as if by magic, but really in the hands of a gopher).

The Met officer handed a copy to me, which I promptly folded and shoved into my pocket without looking at it as he stamped our flight plan. I was about to give him a few parting shots, but Jim, Didier, and the others escorted me out, and I went back to Room No. 1, presenting the gentlemen there with a stamped flight plan.

Our flight plan from Calcutta to Bombay—finally stamped.

With all the proper documents in hand, and our flight plan filed, we piled into the truck for the ride back to our airplane. Sacred cows milled around outside the airport building where all of these conversations took place. They were inside the airport perimeter fence and were the ones we dodged in our wild jeep ride to the bank. Jim and I wondered how they kept the sacred cows off the active runway. We certainly hoped they did, as it would ruin our takeoff if we ran into one.

When we arrived back at the airplane, Jim told me that the two uniformed airline gentlemen who had entered the Met office were a Soviet Aeroflot crew and were absolutely astounded to find Americans there—particularly a woman—for a briefing.

They obviously spoke little English and must have been quite surprised, not only to see a bunch of French and American pilots, but also to witness a female pilot, in the middle of the night, verbally punch out the weatherman.

I admitted that I was definitely not on my best behavior that night. I rarely misbehave like that, but it was just so frustrating! Calcutta, like Bangkok, had taken a long time—not three hours and forty minutes—but much longer than necessary.

Dawn broke as we left Calcutta for Bombay, and the weather was clear all the way, though we had some headwinds, as usual. We left Calcutta at 05:30. The controller was allowing departures on 19L and 01R, and there was quite a bit of traffic. The controller had a disturbing habit of yelling into the transmitter.

One time, when he gave some assurance over the radio, one of the airline pilots replied, "I bet!" The controller was not amused. We departed westbound and climbed only to 8,000 feet because of the strong headwinds. Would we ever have tailwinds?

We flew on G-450 all the way to Bombay. India is not beautiful from 8,000 feet in March. Because it was immediately preceding the monsoon season, the countryside was extremely dry, and a haze layered the land. Nevertheless, the place had its own kind of beauty. We were surprised to see that a great number of irrigation projects had been developed in which to store water for agricultural purposes.

The landscape as we approached Bombay was interesting. There were tall stands of rocks, somewhat similar to Monument Valley, and flat plains. The outskirts of Bombay were sparsely populated, but we then crossed over a portion of the city, which was heavily populated, then over another strip of water, and finally to the area of the airport, located on a small peninsula off the coast.

As we neared the airport, we could see hundreds or thousands of small shacks whose roofs almost overlapped. It was obvious that this was an extremely poor section of the city.

We were embarrassed to find that we landed in Bombay with only 10 gallons (thirty minutes) of fuel left. We never allow that to happen, and it is far below the one-hour reserve that we always maintain. To avoid this difficulty, it would have been necessary to stop in Nagpur. We had opted to go on because we thought we were in better shape. Bad headwinds do exhaust fuel rapidly!

We became concerned about the low fuel situation before we landed and were thinking about all of the possibilities that would be dangerous for us: go-arounds, bad weather, holding, having to divert. They never came to pass. We were vectored for a straight-in to the ILS, runway 27. Piece of cake. What a relief.

The total flight time was six hours and four minutes. We landed at 12:14 on March 19, 1987.

17

Bombay

Thursday, March 19, 1987

In terms of population, Bombay is the second largest city in India, only exceeded by Calcutta. It is the most cosmopolitan and has more skyscrapers than any other city in India. At least two-thirds of its population is concentrated on Bombay Island, which is surrounded on the west and south by the Arabian Sea and on the north and east by Bassein Creek.

In 1996, the government renamed the city of Bombay to the native name Mumbai, after the Koli native Marathi people's Goddess Mumbadevi. When we were there, it was still Bombay.

Bombay was selected by the East India Company for its headquarters in 1672 and continued in that role until 1858. While we were there, we visited the Gateway of India, a monument built on the shores of the Arabian Sea to commemorate the city's role as the principal Indian port and other places of interest including the Taj Mahal Palace Hotel, the Rajabai Clock Tower, and a beautiful mosque, to which there is only access at low tide.

Many citizens of Bombay are poor. Squatters' huts abound alongside the streets, in vacant lots, along ditches that are open sewers, and against most buildings. Living conditions for these people are appalling. We saw one family, evidently newly arrived in the city, setting up housekeeping beside a busy intersection. They were living in a makeshift tent made out of torn and dirty cloth and had no possessions of any consequence.

In Bombay, the processing was speedy and organized. We were escorted to the VIP lounge and simply moved down a row of desks, signing papers and paying fees as we went. There were refreshments and then a short wait, as there was some discussion as to how we were to leave the airport. Our luggage had to go one way, and we had to go another, meeting outside the gate. We had to leave by a particular gate, but we were chauffeured around, and there was little hassle.

We drove a long way to the Centaur Hotel on Juhu Beach. Some of the competitors stayed at the Holiday Inn Juhu Beach and some at the Centaur. Evidently, neither hotel was large enough or had enough empty rooms for all of the competitors.

A press conference was held at 6:00 p.m., and a dinner at the Holiday Inn at 8:00 p.m. We learned that the photojournalist, Tim Knatchbull, with *Vail Snail,* Chuck Rosenquist's airplane, was the grandson of Lord Mountbatten, who had been the last Viceroy of India when it was under British control. In August 1979, he had been on the boat with his family when the Irish Republican Army (IRA) had blown it up. His grandfather and twin brother had been killed, and Tim had been badly wounded. Again, history became tangible for us.

Friday, March 20, 1987

The next morning, Jim and I decided to hire a car and see the city. Allen decided to go, as did Jean Le Ber and Jean-Michel Masson. Therefore, we hired two cars for the day. Jim, Allen, and I took the lead car, directing the driver to take us to the Gateway to India.

The driver drove down the coastline and past a mosque, which was out in the sea. We were told that people could walk out to the mosque during low tide, but during high tide the walkway was under water. It was low tide in the morning, and we saw the mosque again, later in the afternoon, when the tide was high, actually covering the walkway.

Our driver drove through different areas of the city on the way to the Gateway to India. There were nice residential streets, poor areas, shopping areas, sights one would expect to see in most cities. There were interesting signs. One read, "Smoking brown sugar will make you impotent," and another read, "Sell a daughter, burn a bride ... why does this show go on and on?" We felt sad, as we knew that, at that time, parents would sometimes sell a daughter and husbands would set fire to her if they no longer wanted her. Seeing the sign and being reminded of this was upsetting to me. There were several areas that were beautiful with fairly modern buildings and many parks with statues.

We arrived at the Gateway to India, a large building with an arch in the center, and it was explained that this was the first thing that ships see when they arrive in Bombay from abroad. Thus, the reason it was named the Gateway to India. There were many ships in the harbor nearby, as well as cruise boats that went out to the elephant caves. We did not go out there, as we were told that it was a half-day trip. The area around the Gateway to India was beautiful, and the Taj Mahal Palace Hotel was across the street.

Jean and Jean-Michel, in the second car, had not arrived yet, even though we had made a slow tour of the Gateway to India area. We were about to give them up for lost and head to our car when they arrived, flustered, jumped out of their car, and advised us that they were not going to ride anywhere with that maniac driver again. They said that he had become lost, been involved in two accidents, and thought he was determined to kill them.

They dismissed the driver, telling him that we would all return with our driver or get a cab. We told our driver that we would go to the Taj Hotel for lunch and that he should return in an hour.

We went to the restaurant at the top of the hotel and enjoyed a great lunch with a view. I then went downstairs to the shops and ordered an Indian-style dress made from silky sari material that was to be delivered to our hotel that night at 11:00 p.m.

After lunch, Jean, Jean-Michel, and Jim took a taxi to the airport to refuel the airplanes. Allen and I kept our driver and car. We intended to return to the hotel, particularly since I wanted to sit by the pool and relax for a while, but the driver insisted on stopping at the Hanging Gardens. After we saw them, we were pleased that he had. From this vantage point, we had a good view of Bombay across the harbor.

The gardens were fascinating. They are built over Bombay's water

The Temple of Silence in the Hanging Gardens in Bombay.

supply, and picture-taking in the gardens is prohibited. However, there was a guide of sorts as we entered the garden, and he advised us that we could take pictures, as he was friends with the police, and they would cause us no problem so long as we were with him.

He gave us a guided tour, showing us various points of interest, including the Tower of Silence where, he told us, in the Parsi religion, dead bodies were taken. They were laid atop the tower so that the birds could come and pluck the flesh from the bones. Many trees (topiaries) were shaped like animals—of course I took a picture of a giraffe tree/bush. There also was a big shoe with many children around, and our guide recited, in broken Indian-English, the poem about the old lady who lives in a shoe.

As we left and headed back toward the hotel, we saw Reza in a taxi. As we drew parallel, we motioned for him to dismiss his taxi and come with us, since only Allen and I were in the roomy car and he was alone.

Jim, Jean Le Ber, and Jean-Michel Masson arrived at the hotel shortly after I did, and we all got ready for the official dinner, which was being held at the Indian Flying Club.

Hotel doorman with La Girafe in Bombay.

At some point, I brought La Girafe down to the front of the hotel and convinced the uniformed, turbaned doorman that La Girafe needed to have his picture taken with him. He smiled and was eager to hold La Girafe. Of course, I gave him a small tip as well.

I gave Allen the video camera to take some video of this, which he did briefly. He then took some innocuous pictures of various people walking out of the front door of the hotel. Jean-Pierre Malignon, the photojournalist from the Italian Umberto Sala team, was leaving to play golf, so we took his picture also. It seemed strange to us, since in all parts of Bombay that we had seen, there was nothing even remotely approaching a golf course or an area that looked as though it could support one.

The official dinner that evening was held at the Indian Flying Club, and as we entered, we were all presented with a lei and given either a dot or a streak on our forehead (women received dots and men received streaks) for good luck.

The speeches were formal and short. One of the speakers was Mohini Shroff, governor of the Ninety-Nines, Inc., Indian Section, an international women pilots' association. She also was the honorary secretary of the

Three women pilots: I'm with Claudine Sobol-Oosterlinck (left)
and Mohini Shroff (center), governor of an international women
pilots' association, at the Bombay airport before takeoff.

Indian Women Pilots' Association and cochairman of the World Aviation
Education and Safety Congress.

She presented an award to the three women pilots: Claudine
Sobol-Oosterlinck, Gigliola Scorta (a photojournalist on the Caffè Lavazza
team who also has a pilot's license), and me. She talked to me about the
Ninety-Nines and asked me to promise to join when I returned to California. We exchanged addresses and agreed to keep in touch, which we did
for many years.

Saturday, March 21, 1987

A truck came by the hotel to pick up our luggage. The back of the truck
was open, so we were somewhat concerned about our luggage bouncing
out, but a couple of the Indian men who were loading the truck assured us
that they would sit at the back of the truck to keep the luggage in.

A bus then came to pick us up and take us to the airport. We entered through a special gate and went into the VIP lounge to process out, which was done expeditiously. Our luggage also arrived intact.

Mohini Shroff had come to the airport to see us off and also to have her picture taken with Claudine and me. She told us that if this race were held again in two years, she would like for the three of us to fly as a team.

18

Bombay to Amman

Saturday, March 21, 1987

The next leg of our odyssey was from Bombay, India, to Amman, Jordan, via Karachi, Pakistan; Abu Dhabi, UAE; and Riyadh, Saudi Arabia.

Before departing, it was necessary to deal with the Indian officials and pay the various charges. We ended up with a folder full of forms, documents, and receipts—half in English and half in Hindi—but unintelligible in any language. Official stamps and signatures decorated each page. Fortunately for us, the organization filed the flight plans for the race crews. François, of the organization, told us that no less than seven stamps and signatures were required to file each flight plan. We were happy that it was done for us.

We departed Bombay at 09:56 on the morning of March 21, 1987. Bombay looks quite lovely from the air. Our initial route, at flight level 080, took us by way of Karachi, Pakistan.[10] The weather was good but, as usual, we were confronted with a strong headwind of perhaps 20 knots. *Winged Quest* was the first aircraft in the air. We could clearly see the other participants and observers waving goodbye, so we could not resist dipping our wings in a parting salute.

---

10. G-SW SASRO, then G-SWD, Chor (KE), A-1WD.

The taxi clearance involved taxiing east to runway 14, proceeding up that runway to the intersection of 27/09, and departing to the west on runway 27.

Jim Knuppe's aircraft, *AAAAA-Rent-A-Space*, was fully loaded with fuel. The temperature was already 80 degrees F and the humidity high when we departed. Undoubtedly the temperature had climbed even higher before Jim's airplane took off. Steve Picatti was at the controls. He taxied to the intersection as directed and, when cleared for takeoff, applied full power. Ever so slowly, the airplane gained speed. There was a slight rise in the runway about halfway between the intersection and the end. Once he reached the top of the rise, Steve knew he had a problem.

The airplane was not gaining speed fast enough to reach the speed necessary to take off by the end of the runway! He did not abort. Instead, within a few short yards of the end of the runway, he raised the gear retraction handle.

Since the weight of the airplane was still on the gear, the gear would not retract; however, the gear horn started blowing. At the end of the runway, he did not rotate, but simply allowed the airplane to fly off the end of the runway, a few feet from the ground. Perhaps due to ground effect or luck, the airplane flew—sort of.

The airspeed indicator was still too low to permit Steve to initiate a climb, but it did begin to creep up ever so slowly. As the gear retracted, he banked slightly to the left and raised the nose of the airplane a hair to avoid hitting an apartment building.

Mark Mosier was in the back of the airplane taking video footage. At first, he did not know that anything was wrong, but he got the message when he saw the television antennas passing just underneath the right wing. Once over water, Steve was able to gain sufficient airspeed to continue climbing on course. This was probably the worst close call experienced by any of the crews in the race. It was fortunate that Steve, an experienced pilot, was at the controls.

Many, perhaps most, of the airplanes in the race had sufficient range (fuel) to fly directly from Bombay to Muscat, Oman, where they intended to land at Seeb International for fuel. Theoretically, we also had the range to fly the 900 nautical mile distance. But the forecast called for

30- to 40-knot winds, which would have left us arriving at Seeb with only a small fuel reserve.

After our arrival in Bombay with only 10 gallons left, we opted to take the safer route via Pakistan instead. Claudine, in *Novasam,* flew the direct route at only 100 to 200 feet above the ocean in order to avoid the headwinds. Neither Jim nor I would have felt comfortable flying that low.

Our first fuel stop was Karachi, Pakistan. We had some apprehension about landing in Karachi because, in 1986, the Karachi airport had been the scene of a bloody airline hijacking. Also, we were aware that the Soviets were making air strikes into Pakistan in hot pursuit of Afghanistan freedom fighters seeking refuge in Pakistan.

Jim especially did not like the routing, which took us northeast of Karachi some 130 nautical miles. Apart from the high winds and blowing dust, we experienced no problems during the flight, and we landed at Karachi at 13:15. We had been warned that in Karachi we could expect at least a four-hour fuel stop. I was elected to process the paperwork while Jim arranged for the refueling.

After taxiing to the assigned parking spot, Allen and Jim waited for the fuel truck. A pickup truck approached after perhaps ten minutes, and three men were seated inside. The one seated in the middle spoke perfect English.

"I don't like Pakistan. I want to go to America," he said immediately.

Not wanting to engage in a political discussion with the first person he met in Pakistan, Jim assured him that Pakistan was a good country.

"No," he responded, "there is no work and what there is does not pay enough."

Jim said that he knew nothing about such conditions in Pakistan.

"The American Embassy denied me a visa," he continued. "My brother worked there for a while. When I went through the interview, things went well right to the end. Then when they wanted to know why I wanted to go to the United States, my answer was unsatisfactory. They think I won't return to my country. Can you get me a visa?"

Jim had no satisfactory reply.

The refueling operation went smoothly. However, it was necessary to accompany the manager of the refueling operation to a bank in the terminal. Jim was to pay in US dollars, but the refueling crew received its receipt or proof of delivery and payment in Pakistani currency. The "bank" consisted of a stall in front of the terminal where a money changer operated. Before completing the transaction, Jim had to wait until the banker counted and recounted US dollars for three men who appeared to have just come to town on camels.

I went into the general aviation terminal building through the heavily guarded VIP entrance, as had been suggested by Bernard Lamy. Right beside our airplane, at least four guards were present to monitor the landing and unloading of an airliner. The guards were armed with machine guns as were the guards at the VIP entrance.

I immediately went into the VIP lounge, which was luxurious and cool. It was also empty. Very shortly, a young, official-looking fellow came in and asked if he could assist me. I explained that I was there to obtain fuel, pay the landing fees, file a flight plan, and depart.

I asked him to direct me to the flight information office, and he confidently led me off through one building, then outside and to the second floor of another building. Somehow his English and mine were incompatible, as he took me to the head office of Scandinavian Airlines. I explained to him as best I could that this was not the place I was looking for, and he then tried to take me to the offices of Air France. I kept explaining that I wanted the general flight information office, and finally, after many stops, he took me to the office of the director of the airport.

The airport director told me that he had a son who was studying in the United States, and he had visited there. He was extremely nice and most helpful. He directed one of his employees to run around to obtain the customs clearances and other forms and take me to the bank to get my money changed into local currency so that I could pay the landing fees, which he directed were to be minimal (about $15).

He had a soda brought in so that I could wait in comfort while the papers were being processed. He then took me to the appropriate office to file the flight plan, helped me to get more canned sodas for the trip, and escorted me back out through security.

We learned later that the other crews were charged $150 in handling fees, but we paid none and got the best "handler" of all. We all agreed that

We flew over a military installation in Pakistan.

our stop in Karachi had been a pleasant surprise. The process took about two and a half hours, but at least it was not a big hassle, and the extensive paperwork was primarily done for us. Everyone was extremely friendly and helpful, and other than too many large rifles, it was not as intimidating as we had anticipated.

Winged Quest took to the air at 15:43. Because of the intense headwinds, we had decided to stay low and filed for 4,500 feet. The winds increased in velocity the higher one climbed.

Although the usual flight procedures required us to fly north from Karachi and over the coast of Pakistan, several miles out of our way, the fellow from the flight-planning office said that since we were staying at a low altitude, we really should stay off the coast and take a direct route, for security purposes. He was obviously giving us a direct heading and justifying it by saying that it was for "security purposes." In fact, the Pakistani controllers were great. They simply cleared us direct to Jiwani intersection from Karachi.

Jim was flying this leg. I was looking out the window at what was evidently a large military installation below and began taking pictures. Jim reminded me that they would be sensitive about pictures of their military installations, but we agreed that they would never know.

Bio-France Elevage had been refueled right after our airplane. Since they departed within a few minutes of our departure, we were able to talk to Gilles on the radio. They had to return to Karachi almost immediately to check the gear, as it would not retract properly. After a while, they got it to work and continued on their way.

We were planning to land at Bahrain for fuel or, alternatively, in Dhahran, Saudi Arabia. David Beechcroft-Kay of the *Spirit of Hong Kong* team was going to check with Dhahran to see if there was fuel available. If so, he would have them refuel us quickly so that we could be on our way with minimum delay. He soon let us know that there was no fuel there.

After about three hours, we came within radio transmission range of several of the other airplanes in the race and learned that the airplanes that stopped in Seeb received a rude shock. There were only 50 gallons of fuel available for each airplane.

As we were approaching Seeb, at the tip of Oman, we were advised by the other competitors that there was no fuel at all available in either Bahrain or Dhahran. Jim Knuppe had stopped in Bahrain for fuel and had taken all of the remaining fuel. He had no idea that he was buying all that was available, but that is how it turned out. The word was soon passed to all aircraft over 123.45, our common frequency to avoid Bahrain.

Therefore, we had a choice of landing either at Seeb and taking on minimal fuel or flying on to Abu Dhabi where, we were advised, there was sufficient fuel. Therefore, we decided to land at Abu Dhabi to refuel, although this would now mean that we would have to land one more time between there and Amman. We simply did not have the range to fly from Abu Dhabi to Amman without stopping for additional fuel. The only place between Abu Dhabi and Amman that had fuel available was Riyadh, which was 223 nautical miles out of our way. There was no other alternative, however, so we had to make this additional stop.

Because we were cleared direct to Jiwani VOR, we began our 500 nautical mile flight over water to Seeb and then flew overland to Abu Dhabi.[11] The weather was excellent, although it was hazy. Several of the other

---

11. Our route to Abu Dhabi (I had filed for Bahrain but we amended the clearance en route) was A-1WD Jiwani (JI), then R-462 to Seeb (CT), then B-55 to Abu Dhabi.

airplanes had to stop again in Abu Dhabi for fuel also, because of the lack of fuel in Bahrain.

We landed at Abu Dhabi after nightfall at 19:35. Our good friend, Eric Bostick, the maintenance manager for the Emirates Air Service, was there to meet us. Before we had left Abu Dhabi the first time, he had told us to come back through there, as he still had plenty of 100-octane fuel in drums. I think that he was happy to get rid of it, as he had stocked up just for us, and no other general aviation airplanes came through there.

By the time we landed in Abu Dhabi, I was not feeling well at all, so instead of simply refueling and leaving, we stayed for over an hour. I took a pill to settle my stomach and spent quite a bit of time in the bathroom, but the pill worked rapidly, and I soon felt well enough to go on.

The Comanche, *Le Havre–Normandie*, flown by Michel Cogan-Portnoi, had refueled just before us. Michel said that their Omega navigation system had malfunctioned on the way from Bombay and that they were over the coast of Iran before they realized they were in the wrong place. They immediately did a 180 and got out of there.

On starting the engine after his refueling was completed, Michel determined that a magneto was defective, thus he and his crew elected to stay in Abu Dhabi until morning to make repairs. We also learned that the *Bio-France Elevage* had stopped for repairs in Seeb. Their gear retraction system was still giving them problems.

We took off for Riyadh at 21:20.[12] The Dhahran controller cleared us direct Dhahran to Dammam, which is 75 miles northeast of Riyadh. After departing Abu Dhabi, we had to fly up the Persian Gulf in order to again circumnavigate Qatar, which we were reminded would intercept us, and then we crossed the island of Bahrain to the Saudi coast. About one week after our flight, the Iraqis flew down the Persian Gulf, not 50 miles from our route, to bomb Sirri Island, which is north of Abu Dhabi in the Persian Gulf.

Jim flew from Abu Dhabi to Riyadh, and I was on the radio. Of course he had to fly this leg because he was a male. I could talk on the radio until

---

12. The route was V-400 BELSO, V-100 MOTTA, R-19 Dhahran (DHA), B-58 SILNO, and B-58 to Riyadh.

we began communicating with the Saudis. It was nighttime as we passed over Bahrain and Dhahran. The causeway between Bahrain and the mainland was lit and looked like a pearl necklace. We will never forget the sight.

Both cities were absolutely beautiful, and Dhahran, in particular, looked as though it had actually been designed to look good from the air at night. The lights formed patterns or designs that one's imagination could make into animals or other objects. One looked like a flowering tree, and other light patterns were in the shape of tulips or other flowers.

The controllers on duty at Bahrain and Dhahran were friendly and interested in the race. They were Americans and very professional. What a change from the past several weeks of "Say again! Say again!"

The Bahrain controller said he was originally from Washington, DC. Evidently, he was a casualty of the air traffic controller strike in the US, and after he lost his job, he came to Bahrain. He talked to us for some time, asking about the race and about us.

As we were about to lose contact with him, we heard him telling a Saudi airline pilot about us and the race, and the Saudi pilot subsequently contacted us and chatted with us for a while. It was a nice break in the otherwise stillness of the nighttime flight.

Shortly before arriving in Riyadh, we ran into a storm that was blanketing a large part of Saudi Arabia that night. It was raining hard and quite turbulent. Finally, after much buffeting, we arrived in Riyadh at 24:00.

We landed in Riyadh, and both the organization's King Air and Claudine's airplane, *Novasam,* were there. Claudine was having a difficult time, arguing vehemently with the refueling crew. They told her that in Saudi Arabia women are not allowed to drive, let alone fly an airplane, so since she couldn't fly an airplane, she would not need fuel, and they were not going to refuel her airplane.

After a long delay, much discussion, and intervention by Bernard Lamy, her airplane was refueled, and she was able to fly on.

We entered the beautiful general aviation terminal and were served refreshments in the VIP lounge. Our processing and refueling were relatively simple. Jacques and Reza were sound asleep in chairs in the lounge, and Bernard was on the telephone to various airports, checking up on the airplanes that had not been heard from. We advised him that Gilles's airplane, *Bio-France Elevage*, had been delayed in Seeb with landing gear problems, and *Le Havre–Normandie* was still on the ground in Abu Dhabi, also with problems.

This left only *Le Ber–Masson* missing. No one had heard from Jean-Michel Masson and Jean Le Ber. The *Le Ber–Masson* crew had planned to fly direct from Bombay to Seeb, but they had not yet contacted Seeb. Since they had flown straight over the Indian Ocean from Bombay to Seeb, they should have arrived many hours earlier. We remembered hearing them once early in the flight on the common channel but had not talked to them since.

Since both pilots had become good friends of ours, we were extremely concerned. Bernard also was deeply disturbed, and he had called and sent telexes to all of the control towers in the area.

It subsequently turned out that they had landed at Seeb much earlier, but their identification number had been written down improperly, so instead of F-GENR, they were reported under F-GENP, or something similar. After stopping at Seeb, they had then flown to Kuwait for fuel, and then on to Amman. An ingenious route! In fact, they received an award in Amman for their ingenuity. They also avoided most of the bad weather in Saudi Arabia.

After we were assured they were safe, we left Riyadh for Amman. After only one hour and twenty minutes, we were on our way again. We filed for 8,000 feet because of the strong headwinds.[13] We were very tired, and I still did not feel well.

On departing Riyadh, we were given rather complicated departure instructions from the controller, which we either did not understand or were too tired to copy properly, or both. I miscalculated the first estimate, and we both misunderstood the instructions. In any event, the controller had to help us to get oriented after takeoff. After hearing this exchange, Bernard Lamy came on the radio and said, "Anyone awake in N6113U?" His point was well taken, but soon we were straightened out and flying on to Amman.

We managed to stay awake all night. We left Riyadh at 01:36 and arrived at Marka at 05:45. We were flying at 9,000 feet, and it had been raining as

---

13. The flight route was W-22 Gassim (GAS), G-51 Guriat (GRY), R-52 Qatraneh (QTR), A-52 Queen Alia (QAA), then direct to Marka International Airport, Amman, Jordan.

we left Riyadh. The rain increased, and we subsequently encountered a rather severe rain/sandstorm. As usual, the headwinds were bad, but we flew on to Amman. I dozed off and on initially on this leg of the trip, but woke up each time I had to give position estimates and finally gave up trying to sleep at all.

The weather was terrible. The activity on our stormscope showed intense cells all around us. It was bumpy right down to severe turbulence. Occasionally, we had to reduce to maneuvering speed, 139 knots indicated airspeed in the Cessna 210. It rained hard. We thought that we were again flying through hail, only to find that this time it was a sandstorm. The wind churned up the sand and dust, carrying it to great heights.

Other airplanes had the same problem at much higher altitudes. David Beechcroft-Kay in the *Spirit of Hong Kong* hit a bird at 10,000 feet and landed to find blood and feathers plastered all over the nose of his airplane. Because of the strong headwinds, we had the company of the organization's Beechcraft King Air for virtually the entire flight. Bernard was a great help. He relayed messages for us to the various controllers and, perhaps more importantly, kept us awake.

At about the Saudi/Jordanian border, the storm was finally behind us.

On arriving at Queen Alia VOR (QAA), we asked for vectors to the ILS. The controller concurred and began to direct us to the ILS approach to runway 24. The runway elevation is 2,539 feet. The controller made us stay at 6,000 feet until we were over the threshold and then said, "You are cleared for the approach." Wonderful!

We put down full flaps, lowered the gear, and reduced the power in order to make the runway. It was an elevator approach—straight down! However, we managed to get to the runway with little difficulty except that we left our inner ears at 6,000 feet for a few hours.

We were surrounded by the usual entourage of photographers, organization personnel, and officials of the Jordanian government. In short order, we were processed and were on our way to the hotel for some breakfast and much-needed rest.

19

Amman, Jordan

Sunday, March 22, 1987

Amman is the capital and largest city of Jordan, and the country's economic, political, and cultural center. It is the fifth largest and among the most modernized cities in the Arab world. It initially was built on seven hills, but by the time we were there, it spanned over nineteen hills.

The Hashemite Kingdom of Jordan is a constitutional monarchy that was ruled by King Hussein bin Talal from 1952 until his death on February 7, 1999. His wife, Queen Noor, had been trained as an urban planner and now worked as a philanthropist/world activist. King Hussein's eldest son, Crown Prince Abdullah II bin Al-Hussein, assumed his constitutional powers as Monarch the day his father passed away. He is the forty-first generation direct descendant of the Prophet Muhammad.

We were happy to land in Amman at dawn after another rough overnight flight. Members of the Royal Falcons Acrobatic Team were not only friendly, but also the best greeters we had encountered, and they processed us expeditiously. We appreciated it, as we were absolutely exhausted. We were taken to the Holiday Inn where we immediately fell asleep without even undressing.

We woke to attend a press conference at 5:00 p.m. Ali Ghandour, the chief pilot for the Royal Jordanian Falcons Aerobatic Team, whom we

At the press conference in Amman. Jim and
La Girafe are in the back row.

had met when we landed, spoke, as well as Dr. Ghaith Pharaon, one of
the race sponsors, and, of course, Bernard. He no longer pronounced
public incorrectly.

I was interviewed by a woman reporter from a Jerusalem newspaper
and another woman from a TV station in Amman. We were driven to the
residence of the Italian ambassador for cocktails and dinner, then returned
to the hotel for a drink and, again, we fell into bed, still exhausted.

Monday, March 23, 1987

After breakfast, we decided to go to American Express to exchange our
travelers checks for US dollars, which we needed to pay for our fuel.
Patrick Ducommun from the TDK team asked if he could go with us,
as he also needed to change some money. We arrived at the American
Express office at 9:00 a.m., but were informed that they would not have
any money until 10:30.

Therefore, we had our driver take us to the old Roman amphitheater in central Amman. This amphitheater was built by the Romans in about AD 400 and was in remarkably good condition. Most of it had been preserved, and some parts restored. We could sense the long history of this place.

Afterward, we stopped in a nearby shop, the Syriac Exhibition, and the owner, Abraham Ozgul, was excited to welcome us to his shop, as he had seen us on television. He told us that he had once lived in the United States and had great memories of our country. He was an artist and had made some of the jewelry and dagger cases on display.

He showed us a dagger case made from silver more pure than sterling, ornately designed around some mounted stones. He also had some authentic old Syrian necklaces, which were for sale. I bought an old Syrian necklace, agate and silver, which he said was 110 years old. He gave us a certificate of authenticity.

We then asked our driver to take us to a hill above the city for a panoramic view. From this viewpoint, we could see the city spread out in all directions, with the Roman amphitheater nestled against one hill. He also took us past the area where King Hussein and Queen Noor lived, and also past the home of either the former king or Prince Abdullah.

We returned to the American Express office, and when we tried to cash our travelers checks, they gave us Jordanian currency. We again explained to them specifically that we needed US currency, since we could only pay for fuel in US dollars, but it seemed that they had ignored this. They told us that we could only obtain US currency from a money changer, and they gave us the name of one in downtown Amman.

We went to the money-changing office as we were directed, and from there, we were told to go down a back alley, up two flights of stairs, to another small office. We were taken into a back office, and the person in charge spoke with us for some time about the race, asking many questions. He then filled out many papers and subsequently gave them to someone else and then directed us to go to a small cage in the front office.

We did this, gave them our signed travelers checks, and they gave us some more papers to take to a larger cage in that same office. This had all taken a great deal of time, since no one filled out or signed papers quickly.

When we finally were given our money at the main cage, it was again

Jim and I are with Royal Jordanian pilots.

in Jordanian currency. By this time, we were quite impatient and insisted that we receive US currency, since we had been clear from the beginning that this was what we wanted. We returned again to the first fellow in the back room, and he apologized for his mistake, saying that he was so interested in hearing what we were saying that he had inadvertently neglected to indicate that we were to get US dollars. He filled out a set of corrected papers, and after going through the entire process again, we finally obtained the US currency.

We arrived back at the hotel with just sufficient time to change clothes and leave for the airfield where King Hussein and Queen Noor were hosting a reception for us. I had been told that I should wear a dress or skirt instead of slacks, but I did not have anything clean. There was a small shop at the hotel where I purchased the only piece of clothing they had which would be appropriate.

We arrived at the airfield at 3:00 p.m. There were comfortable chairs set up in front of the Royal Jordanian Falcons' hangar, with one row of cushioned chairs, carpeting, and a table with a large flower arrangement

King Hussein and Queen Noor. Jim and I are in the background.

for the King, Queen, and their family. A small orchestra toward the right side of the chairs kept us entertained for approximately an hour while we waited for the King and his family to arrive.

Prior to the King's arrival, I had distributed raisins, almonds, raisin hats, and other gifts to all of the guests and their children who had been included in the festivities, and they were enjoying the treats when the King and Queen arrived. We were informed that the miniseries *Fresno* was currently playing in Amman, and many people asked whether the raisins were from the Kensingtons or "from the good guys or the bad guys." Of course we said they were from the good guys.

The extended royal family, including quite a few more children, arrived first, and King Hussein and Queen Noor arrived at about 4:20 p.m. The King was driving his Mercedes and, of course, they were escorted by security personnel. A fantastic aerobatic air show put on by three pilots in Pitts aircraft commenced almost immediately. Afterward there was a performance by some folk dancers.

The King's eldest son, Prince Abdullah, and I spoke for quite a while.

He was a nice young man, about nineteen years old, and very friendly. He asked a lot of questions about the race so far and was interested in our various airplanes. He said that he was a helicopter pilot and would be flying his helicopter to accompany our airplanes as we took off to leave Amman. He looked forward to doing that and being a part of our adventure.

I asked him if he expected to be the king one day, and he said that he had absolutely no interest in politics or becoming king and would like to just fly. I reminded him that his father, King Hussein, was also an experienced pilot. He said that his father could do both, but he really did not want to be king—just fly.

After the entertainment, the King presented the awards for first place, second place, and third place. There was only six minutes' difference between the times of the first and second airplanes, which was amazing for a leg of thirteen hours. *Italia Wings*, whose pilots, Mauro Masson and Claudio Soro, both Alitalia captains, had become good friends of ours, prevailed over *Microjet-Mammouth,* the Wassmer 421, which was slower but had a range of sixteen and one-half hours and did not need to stop to refuel.

Jean-Michel and Jean Le Ber received an award for the most creative flight—they flew through and landed in Kuwait, which none of the other competitors had done. I had been told that I was to receive some award from King Hussein, and Bernard said that I should take La Girafe with me when I went to meet him. I had explained the relevance of La Girafe to the Chief of Protocol and told him about Valley Children's Hospital.

The King asked me to come forward, and he presented me with a beautiful Longines watch with the Jordanian royal crest on it with a gold-and-leather watchband. I was happy to receive it, not only because it was beautiful but also, when I was buying watches for everyone in our family in Singapore, I had forgotten to buy one for myself.

The award was one that was probably dreamed up by Bernard as an excuse to get an interesting picture of me and La Girafe with the King. The King announced that the award was for my "always-present smile" and for "boosting the spirit and morale of the group." I introduced La Girafe to the King, who shook hands with him for the photographers.

As I turned to return to my seat, the King's youngest daughter, Princess

La Girafe and I are receiving a gift from
King Hussein at an airport ceremony.

Iman, came toward me to see the giraffe. I bent down and she petted and hugged the giraffe. I thought for a while that I might have a difficult time extricating the giraffe, but finally she was distracted and went back to her seat with no further problems.

King Hussein and Queen Noor then stood together and shook hands with all of the competitors. Afterward, we adjourned to an excellent array of food, beautifully prepared and displayed, inside the hangar. King Hussein and Queen Noor came to speak with me, and they asked about Valley Children's Hospital. The Queen requested a pledge form and said that they may make a small donation.

Later on, I was standing by our airplane when the King and Queen came by to look at the various airplanes. Queen Noor stopped and spoke with me for a while, telling me that she was born in the United States and had spent some time in Santa Monica when she was a child. Since I was one of two women pilots (the other was French and more reticent

I showed La Girafe to Princess Iman. The Queen is seated at the left.

to talk), we spent quite a bit of time together as we walked among the other competitors' airplanes.

Queen Noor is a beautiful lady, elegant, genuine, and she seemed to be sincerely interested in us and the race. She was formerly Lisa Halaby, the daughter of Najeeb Halaby, who was the CEO and chairman of Pan American World Airways.

Everyone was curious about our airplanes, and in addition to the officials and personnel from the Royal Jordanian Falcons, other people from the city had been invited to this reception. One fellow, Mustafa Hudhud, the general manager of a building material supply business, had brought his son, Fadi, to see us. Fadi, as well as his father, were evidently intrigued by airplanes and flying. They requested that we allow Fadi to sit in the airplane, which we did, and of course I took his picture.

That evening, the official dinner was held in the hotel and sponsored by Alia, the Royal Jordanian airline. It had been a beautiful and event-filled day, but we were happy that there were not too many long speeches and we were able to get to bed fairly early.

Jim (left) and Bruno
Lamy dressed for the
reception in Amman.

I was dressed up for the
reception and posed in front
of this photo of the King.

Tuesday, March 24, 1987

We left Amman in two buses early in the morning for Petra, over an hour's drive to the south. Petra is one of the most incredible places I have ever seen. Whenever anyone asks me where I would like to return to someday, the first place I think of is Petra.

I still get goosebumps whenever I think of it. This city, full of temples, theaters, gardens, tombs, villas, and Roman baths, was at one time the crossroads between East and West. It was built by the Nabateans in 400 BC and at its apex was home to about 30,000 people. It continued to thrive after the Roman Empire annexed it in the second century AD. The Romans simply administered the city and did not "conquer" it.

A large amphitheater that appeared to be Roman may have been built during this period. It continued to thrive until a large earthquake struck. Then the trade routes shifted, and by the middle of the seventh century, what remained of Petra was largely deserted, though it still was inhabited by a group of Bedouins who lived in some of the caves.

The buses parked at the entrance to a nice hotel, and we had refreshments before going into the ruins. From the hotel, we walked down a path, past Bedouin tents, to an area where numerous horses were grazing or trotting around in a small valley.

The guides, in long robes and Bedouin headdresses, caught the horses and brought them to the edge of a platform. We were expected to mount the platform and then the horse. For some of the competitors who were not riders, including Jim, this platform was a great help.

Jim was not at all certain that he would be riding a horse on this day, as he did not like horses and had only ridden once before in his life. That time, he had fallen off. However, his interest in seeing Petra outweighed his fear and distrust of horses, so he bravely agreed to ride one. It was expected that the guides would lead the horses down the pathway toward the ruins, which also was reassuring for Jim.

I was given my first pony at the age of five and had ridden all of my life, so I did not need the assistance. I found a particularly spirited horse and persuaded the guide to let me mount from the ground, instead of from the platform. I also convinced him that I knew how to ride a horse and did not need to be led. There was no bridle, rather a single rope attached to the halter, and the guide handed me the rope and encouraged me to walk, trot, or canter as I wished, while he ran alongside.

This beautiful and spirited Arabian horse was eager and wanted to go, but I felt constrained to hold him back because I did not wish to wear out my poor guide who was running alongside and obviously becoming weary. He finally mounted another horse and rode along beside me, his robes flying out behind him as we galloped along the gravel path between the rock cliffs and around young schoolgirls and the other competitors, whose guides still were leading them at an ambling walk.

Called the Siq, the main entrance to Petra is a natural ravine that splits the towering rocks for almost a mile.

Once we made our way through the Siq, we emerged into a clearing, and I pulled my horse to a stop, drew in my breath, and stared, wide eyed, with goosebumps. Before us was the most incredible, perfectly beautiful, most

I chose a spirited horse to ride into Petra.

Jim on horseback (front right) with side walkers/
guides for the tour of Petra.

dramatic structure in Petra—Al-Khazneh, or the Treasury. It is a fantastic building more than 100 feet high, its facade with two levels of columns and statues etched into the face of the mountain. It was carved out of sandstone so fine that it appeared to be marble. Steps led to the main entrance, between large round columns.

It was breathtaking and in stark contrast to the surrounding rugged cliffs. I dismounted and waited for Jim. Dismounting, for Jim, was going to be a chore, so of course I filmed it. He was really a good sport and did well. We went inside the temple, where we gazed at the beautifully colored stone and perfectly formed rooms. This is truly one of the Seven Wonders of the World.

The Siq is the main entrance to view the ancient city of Petra.

There was a camel in the open area in front of the Treasury, and as a typical tourist, I had to ride it. One mounts a camel when it is sitting down, rather close to the ground, and then the camel stands up. This is not terribly difficult (for me, maybe for the camel), and it also is not difficult to stay on and ride comfortably. However, in order for me to dismount, the camel must again descend to his knees. This is an extremely jerky motion, as the camel first kneels, and the back of the saddle digs into one's back, and then the back end of the camel goes down, so one is again in a level position. I could not imagine that there was any way that this could be done gracefully. I certainly felt anything but graceful.

After exploring this area for a time, we were directed to remount our horses and continue on to another area. Nearly everyone had departed, and I could not find my horse or my guide. I finally saw him up on a hill, kneeling on a prayer rug, facing Mecca and praying. I waited until his

In Petra—Al-Khazneh, or the Treasury, a temple was etched into the face of a mountain.

prayers were completed, and then he brought my horse and we continued on to join the rest.

We explored many places. We rode on to the amphitheater area and stopped briefly. It had been built by the Romans who had always been known for their amphitheaters. We then continued on to another area containing a number of cave homes and another temple, high on a cliff. Leaving horses and guides below, we ascended the long staircase and explored the area, then stood for a while on the edge of the cliff, looking out over the panorama of rocks, cave homes, flat desert, and beautifully carved sandstone buildings. This was truly a magnificent place, and I wanted to stay longer.

I descended down to my horse and guide and began the return trip to the buses. We galloped along together, his robes blowing behind him, with him occasionally chattering in Arabic or broken English. I allowed my mind to wander and imagined that we were back in the days of Petra's glory, two Nabateans, riding along on our Arabian horses and enjoying the scenery on a beautiful spring day.

It was difficult to break the spell, but we finally arrived at the dismount area, and I reluctantly gave up my wonderful, spirited horse who had become my Nabatean family. There was just no way to squeeze him onto our airplane. The organizers had paid for the excursion, but I wanted to give my guide something extra. First of all, because he had allowed me to ride by myself, which the other competitors had not been allowed to do. And second, because he had obtained an extra horse for

I rode a camel in Petra.

himself so that we could gallop instead of walk, which was magical for me. He had helped transport me to another long-ago time.

I had no money, so I had to wait until Jim, with his guide, rode (and walked) up. We walked back to the hotel, where a cool drink and nice buffet awaited, and then returned to our buses.

The return trip to Amman was not only long, but stressful. The bus was traversing a narrow two-lane road with occasional detours for construction, and the traffic was bumper to bumper, with many trucks interspersed among the cars. Ours was primarily the nonsmoking bus except for a couple of smokers at the back, but about one-third of the way to Amman, the other bus had a flat tire.

We stopped at a crossroads containing a service station and small grocery store of sorts, and most of us went to the grocery store to find something cold to drink while the tire was being repaired. The locals in the store seemed amazed by this invasion of French, Americans, and Italians, as they obviously had not seen many foreigners in this small, crossroads community.

It began to rain, so we returned to the vicinity of the buses. Children darted out from behind the buildings, danced around, and made noise to make themselves seen, and then shyly ducked behind each other or the buildings again. We were all still in fairly high spirits, and Patricia was "dancing in the rain" with one of the organization pilots outside of our bus. The tire repair seemed to be more complicated than anticipated, so it was decided that all of the competitors would climb aboard our bus to return to the hotel.

I had tried to be tolerant of the smokers throughout the trip, but the remaining bus trip to Amman was more than I could stand. Some of the smokers puffed nonstop, and in a small, crowded bus the air was soon unbearable. I began to get a headache, then sick to my stomach, and finally, when Regis, two seats behind us, lit up, I turned around and tearfully asked him not to smoke. I explained to Umberto Sala, who had been sitting in the seat ahead of me and smoking, that I was allergic to smoke, which gave me a horrible headache, and that at this point, I was going to simply have to request that people stop smoking.

Many other nonsmokers had been grumbling about the smoke as well, and the driver had turned the fans on to try to keep the air moving, so the bus became rather cold. The smokers quit, for the most part, although there were a couple of women in the front of the bus who were not with our group but some sort of guides who never did get the message and never did stop. It was a horrible trip back to the hotel, and I had a huge headache by the time we arrived.

20

Amman to Rome

Wednesday, March 25, 1987

We left the hotel in the morning for the airport, but there were many delays before we could depart. Jim and I were supposed to be the seventh airplane to leave, but our flight plan had somehow not been processed in a timely manner, so we were second or third from the last.

Two helicopters, one piloted by Prince Abdullah, escorted the first four airplanes down the runway and off into the sky until they nearly disappeared from view. They planned to escort all of the airplanes, but the fifth airplane was the Cathay Pacific team flying the Martell-sponsored airplane. Since alcohol is not permitted, officially, in Jordan, the helicopter escort ended.

Most of the crews obtained permission to overfly Syria. However, we did not want to land in Damascus if we were experiencing mechanical or other problems. This reasoning turned out to be fortuitous. It was impossible to cross Israel at that time. Anyone crossing Israel, even assuming permission could be obtained, would have made it impossible for a race event of this type to ever occur again, and, of course, the aircraft and crew making the crossing would have been permanently enjoined from ever again crossing or entering an Arab country.

Prince Abdullah piloted a helicopter as he
escorted a departing race airplane.

Bernard Lamy stressed these points during our briefing the night
before we left Amman. To my knowledge, none of the airplanes violated
the prohibition against crossing Israel.

At 12:45 we departed Amman with Jim flying. When we finally took off,
the weather was clear and beautiful. We had planned to fly south from
Amman to the tip of the Sinai, then north across the Gulf of Suez, across
Cairo, and proceed across the Mediterranean to Rhodes. However, it was
not to be. Again, because of our old nemesis, the headwinds, we calculated that we would have insufficient fuel, and therefore we elected to
stop in Cairo, even though Jim had vowed that he would rather swim than
stop in Cairo again.[14]

From Amman, we flew south across the desert until we reached the
head of the Gulf of Aqaba, where the cities of Aqaba, Eilat, and Sharm el
Sheikh join the countries of Saudi Arabia, Israel, and Egypt, and where

---

14 Our actual course was A-52 Qatraneh (QTR), R 52 Aqaba (AQB), W-727 Ras Nasrani
   (RAN), and A-411 to Cairo.

begins the northeast edge of the Sinai Peninsula. We sidestepped Eilat, Israel, and took up a course over the Gulf of Aqaba along the Sinai coastline, with Saudi Arabia on our left and the Sinai Peninsula to the right, avoiding a restricted area in Saudi Arabia.

When passing over Aqaba, we remembered reading how Lawrence of Arabia had led an army across the desert to attack Aqaba from the land side, where it was largely undefended, rather than from the sea, where it was heavily fortified. The result was a complete rout of the more numerous Turkish defenders. History is constantly visible here.

The scenery was spectacular, and the contrast between the deep blue water of the Gulf of Aqaba and the dryness of the Sinai Peninsula was striking. The Sinai (about 23,000 square miles) is a triangular desert peninsula that forms a land bridge between Africa and Asia in northeast Egypt. It is bordered by the Gulf of Suez on the southwest, the Red Sea on the south, the Gulf of Aqaba on the southeast, and the Mediterranean Sea on the north. We had always thought of the Sinai as being a desert, but there are mountains reaching to over 8,000 feet.

As we rounded the lower end of the Sinai Peninsula and headed northwest, we wondered aloud why the Sinai was such a point of controversy or a battleground. It seemed to be rough and rugged and appeared to be uninhabited. Perhaps nomads live there, but there were few settlements visible from the air. We next flew over the Suez, but could not see as far north as the canal before we entered the air space over Egypt and flew on toward Cairo. We landed in Cairo at 16:20. We assumed that it would take forever to get processed, but we had no choice.

This Cairo stop was not nearly as long or expensive as our last one on the way to Abu Dhabi had been. We immediately asked for Egypt Air to be our handling agent, so we were processed quickly, filed our flight plan, paid our landing fee (only $135 this time), and were off. I did the paperwork while Jim refueled. It seemed to speed things up somewhat, as a woman doing the paperwork was an oddity and the officials seemed eager to cooperate with me. Within a couple of hours, we were ready for takeoff with our friends in *Bio-France Elevage* immediately behind us.

I was flying and Jim was in the right seat and on the radio as we climbed out to the west en route to El Daba, where we would proceed

The Sinai.

across the Mediterranean, now intending to stop at Athens for fuel before proceeding to Rome, our next mandatory stop. We were looking forward to a beautiful flight.

When we reached altitude, I leaned the mixture to the top of the green or 120 pounds per hour, which is recommended by the manufacturer. Suddenly, the engine sputtered and sounded as though it would stop. The fuel flow was still at the top of the green, however the TIT (the Turbo Intake Temperature gauge, which replaced the Exhaust Gas Temperature gauge on the airplane) was going over redline. This was not good!

When an engine stops running, pilots are trained to take a series of steps, beginning with checking the circuit breakers on the left and ending with pushing in the mixture control to enrich the mixture on the right. While I checked the circuit breakers on my left, Jim immediately enriched the mixture, increasing the fuel flow (on the right), and this brought the TIT gauge down. The engine ran smoothly again. I again tried to lean the mixture. *Cough, cough, sputter, sputter, pause.* Again, I enriched the mixture, and the engine ran smoothly again. We speculated that the turbocharger may have malfunctioned.

Jim calculated that we were burning more than 20 gallons of fuel (per hour) with the mixture full rich, and at that rate, we could possibly reach Rhodes, but certainly not Athens. However, even if we theoretically had sufficient fuel, it did not take long for us to decide that it would not be a good idea to continue across the Mediterranean Sea in the dark. No pilot would choose to fly across the Mediterranean in daytime, let alone in the dark, with an engine that obviously had a problem.

Night would be falling shortly, and with our engine in this condition, we knew that we had a major problem. Reluctantly, we turned back toward Cairo.

Jim called Cairo and told them of our problem. He suggested that it might be a real good idea for them to give us vectors back to Cairo. The controller quickly agreed, and we turned around to the assigned heading and returned to Cairo for a night landing at Cairo International, an airport with which we were all too familiar.

On our first landing in Cairo en route to China, we were directed to the isolated parking area and had to be transported back and forth to the terminal via a small bus. On the second landing, which had gone relatively well, we were allowed to park at the base of the tower. On this occasion, we requested the base of the tower, but were directed to the remote parking area by a "follow me" jeep.

Remote was hardly the word for it—we were almost back in Sinai. We explained our problem to the driver, and he promised to send someone from Egypt Air maintenance immediately. In addition, we also had contacted Egypt Air directly and requested that they send someone to assist us.

We thought that we had explained exactly where we were parked, but after the "follow me" jeep had gone and no one had returned to us for over a half hour, we contacted Egypt Air by Unicom again. They still could not find us, and it probably was an hour and a half before they finally arrived. By this time, it was very dark, and we thought we might have to spend the night in the airplane in the remote parking area, forgotten by the world, except for the occasional guard who patrolled the area.

After some delay, the Egypt Air representative found us. He said that a mechanic who could work on the airplane was scheduled to come to work the following morning and gave us the name of the mechanic who he said we should contact. All of the mechanics had gone home for the evening, and there would be no way to get our airplane repaired that night. There was nothing to do but go to a hotel. They finally sent a bus for us, and, after more delay, we were taken to the main terminal to process out through customs. We took all of our luggage because for security reasons, we were afraid to leave the luggage—any of it—in the airplane.

We had requested that Egypt Air act as our agent, but the personnel this evening were not nearly as efficient as the ones we had that afternoon. They did not seem to know how to get things accomplished and told us that it was much more difficult to process through, since we were going out of the terminal to a hotel. We had Egyptian visas, however, and later thought that if we had simply gone through the regular customs procedure, we may have been able to process through more quickly.

The fact that we had arrived by private airplane created some difficulties because we did not have a flight number and were not passengers regularly scheduled to enter. The personnel trying to process us continued to request our flight number, as they thought that we must have come by a commercial airline. They had no plan for processing through pilots who flew general aviation airplanes.

After about two hours, I began to get impatient. I first called over a man who appeared to be the official in charge of customs. I explained to him what had occurred and told him that if he could not get us processed through immediately, I would like to speak to the airport manager. I asked him for the airport manager's name and where his office was located. He would not, of course, give this information to me, and he soon disappeared again on the other side of the separating fence, never to be seen again.

I then spied a room with a sign "Press" above it. I went in, and two or three people were present, whom I suspected were journalists. I explained the problem to them and my frustration, and the fact that we had been in Cairo for nearly five hours and had been unable to get out of the airport due to the bureaucracy. They sympathized. However, they also had no immediate remedy, though they were interested in talking about the air race. I thought that, if nothing else, they would report something about the pilots who were stuck in limbo at the airport. What a mess!

Our agents from Egypt Air reappeared, and we finally were able to exit the airport. It was midnight before we arrived at the Heliopolis Sheraton, which was only 4 or 5 miles from the airport. We had a light dinner and went to bed immediately after first calling Bernard Lamy in Rome to let him know that we were safe but had a problem.

Thursday, March 26, 1987

The next morning, Jim and I arose early, and after a quick breakfast we called Egypt Air and asked for the mechanic whose name had been given to us. We were advised that he was out of town until Saturday. We did reach another man, however, Ali El Sukari who said he was a mechanic and would meet us when we arrived at the airport and would assist us. He told us where to meet, and we left for the airport at 7:00 a.m. Allen remained at the hotel with our luggage.

When we arrived at the airport, no one knew where this particular meeting place was. We knew the general area, but not the exact gateway, so after trying three or four entrances, we again phoned Mr. Sukari, and after some fits and starts, he found us.

The next problem to solve was how to get back onto the airport tarmac. Returning to our airplane was not a simple task. We did not know how long it would take to fix the problem. Thus, we opted to get a temporary pass to enter the airport and not to process all of our luggage through or clear customs and immigration until we knew for sure that the matter would be promptly repaired and that we would not have to spend another night in Egypt.

Mr. Sukari took us to the office where permits were issued. This involved walking up dark stairs and through long hallways to the appropriate office. The official who ran that office said that he must receive a letter from another airport official before he could act. Back down the hallways and stairs we went, to the appropriate official's office. Though troubled by this extra work, he graciously wrote the letter in long hand and applied the appropriate stamp to the bottom near his signature to make it official.

Then back we went to the office where the badges were issued. The man in charge signed the appropriate form to have the badges issued, and then we went to another office where the badges were physically issued, presented the paper, and only then did we receive the coveted badges. Finally, we obtained a temporary pass to go onto the tarmac to our airplane. Even with Mr. Sukari's assistance, it took approximately two hours of going from office to office, getting paperwork, signatures, and stamps.

The last stamp that we were required to obtain was the one that allowed us to go through the gate. We needed to go through Gate 33, to the Egypt Air maintenance facility. However, the fellow behind the desk advised us that he did not have a stamp for Gate 33. Therefore, he stamped our papers with the stamp for Gate 35.

We then walked with Mr. Sukari out to the front of the main terminal building en route to the gates near the shop where we hoped to be admitted to the airport. We went to the gate for the Egypt Air maintenance, Gate 33, where everyone, of course, knew Mr. Sukari, who was in charge of maintenance there. When they saw our papers, however, they would not allow us to enter, as our papers were stamped Gate 35.

Mr. Sukari explained to the guards that the person who stamped our papers simply did not have a stamp for Gate 33, but that we needed to go to Egypt Air maintenance, and that obviously we could go to Gate 35, enter there legally, and walk back to the maintenance area (approximately an extra three blocks each way), or he could simply allow us to go through directly. Of course he would not allow us to do this, so we had to walk the extra three blocks to Gate 35, where we entered and walked three blocks back to Egypt Air maintenance inside Gate 33.

All of the gates are guarded by armed guards. We had an uneasy feeling about passing through the gate, because we were not sure about the training these guards had. In any event, we were permitted to pass without being shot.

Jim knew generally what the problem with the fuel flow and engine was from his telephone conversation the previous evening with the general manager of Executive Wings, Inc., of Fresno, California, who told him that he thought the fuel injectors to the cylinders and the fuel filters were clogged. He said that when the fuel system was in this condition, some of the cylinders were being starved for fuel when the mixture was leaned.

Mr. Sukari and another mechanic went with us out to the airplane, and they quickly removed the cowling and began to tear down the engine to the extent required to clean the fuel injectors and the fuel filters right there on the tarmac at the isolated parking area. Shortly, a man driving a small electric tractor pulled up. It had American flag decals on the sides, and the driver introduced himself as an American, working for and maintaining the airplanes for the American Embassy in Cairo. He spoke with Mr. Sukari and the other mechanic, and then returned to get his tools and an air compressor, and the three mechanics set about doing the work.

Apparently, we had picked up sand in the fuel injectors when we had flown through the sandstorm between Riyadh and Amman. Among the three mechanics, they took our engine apart, blew the dirt and sand out of the fuel injectors, cleaned the fuel filters, and put the airplane back together in less than two hours.

When it appeared as though everything was under control, I left and went back to the hotel to collect Allen and our suitcases. We agreed to meet at the entrance to the main terminal, as we would all have to process through customs again. We were hoping that it would not take a long time to do so, but we were not optimistic.

Jim had ordered fuel. In short order, the dirty injectors and filters had been cleaned, the aircraft had been refueled, and we were ready to depart, except for clearing up a few matters with immigration, customs, and paying the fuel bill. Jim did not have enough dollars to pay for the fuel and told the fuel truck manager that he would pay him when I returned with money. Mr. Sukari instructed him to fill the airplane. After it was filled, two fellows who worked on the fuel truck, the fuel truck manager and his helper, accompanied Jim everywhere until they were paid.

Jim tried to pay the mechanic from Egypt Air, but he would not accept any payment. Jim paid his helper a few dollars. He gave Mr. Sukari a pen set, but he was not seeking any kind of payment at all and was reluctant to accept the gift. Without Mr. Sukari's help, we would still be wandering around the Cairo International Airport. Jim did not give anything to the American mechanic but his thanks, and he seemed happy with that.

When Jim returned to the terminal to wait for me, he was accompanied by the two men from the fuel truck. They were not going to let Jim out of their sight until they had been paid. If Jim sat down, they sat down. If Jim stood up, they stood up. If Jim walked around, they walked with him. The fuel manager was just as happy to see me as Jim was. He was quickly paid and was on his way.

Allen and I arrived with the luggage and entered the terminal building. I requested a handling agent from Egypt Air, and a tall, elegant gentleman with a three-piece suit soon appeared and introduced himself as Mr. Hassam, the managing director of Egypt Air. Jim had joined Allen and me by that time, and Mr. Hassam escorted the three of us through the first security area to his private office. He told Jim and Allen to wait in his office and offered them tea. He instructed me to accompany him to do the necessary paperwork. This he did with much gallantry and flourish.

He told me immediately that he did not customarily act as a handling agent, but he had read about us and seen us on TV, and he was particularly impressed that I was a woman pilot. He thought that I was extremely brave and courageous and evidently worth his time.

Whenever we would approach a security area or an office, he would take my elbow, guide me ahead of him, and say, "After you, Captain," loudly enough for everyone present to hear. We immediately were cleared. He convinced the officials that we should not have to pay any landing fee at all, but rather only an overnight parking fee of $8. This was the extent of our payment that day, because the mechanics with Egypt Air also would not accept any payment for their assistance, though we tried hard to give them something.

I gave Mr. Hassam my card, and he was going to give me his, though it was written in Arabic. We were just going out to the gate to leave, so he did not have time to write the English translation on it. He kissed my hand gallantly and expressed his pleasure in assisting me. We think that he really did enjoy it, particularly when a woman stopped me in the airport and asked for my autograph, explaining that she had seen me on TV and that I "looked the same in English as I did in Arabic!"

Without Mr. Hassam's help, we would probably still be wandering around the airport. Even with his help, it took quite some time to finish the processing, pay all of the fees, and file a flight plan. Prior to actually filing

Leaving Cairo after mechanical repairs and flying over the Pyramids.

the flight plan, we received a weather briefing, which generally showed good weather for our route to Athens.[15]

We finally left Cairo, without a test flight, on March 26, 1987, at 15:30, Jim piloting and me in the right seat, and this time flying over the city and the pyramids before heading to El Daba and across the Mediterranean. Of course, I took a picture of the pyramids from above.

We had been somewhat concerned about flying across the Mediterranean without flight-testing the airplane after it had been repaired, but the airplane continued to perform well. The sun had set over the Mediterranean, this time outlining the mountains of Crete in gold before disappearing into the sea. Jim and I felt a twinge of sadness at this sunset, as we knew that it would be the last one of the air race.

Athens at night was spectacular. There were many boats and yachts in the harbor, and their lights were reflected in the water. We could see the

15. We filed for flight level 080, and the route was R-778 Fayoum (FYN), which was inoperative, W-727 El Daba (DBA), B-12 Sitia (SIT), A-14 Milos (MIL), then Athens Control gave us B-34 FALCO direct Athens.

Acropolis in the distance and the sparkling lights of the city all around. We landed in Athens at 19:40 without further incident.

To say that Athens was the most efficient airport that we visited is a great understatement. The people at the FBO in Athens were tremendous, and the bureaucracy was nonexistent. They have the processing of transit aircraft down to a science. We taxied up in front of a modern building on a well-lighted ramp. The fuel truck immediately pulled up in front of the airplane and started the refueling process while we were driven to the building, less than one block away, for the payment of landing fees and other miscellaneous charges, all of which were reasonable. They also were hospitable and made us a cup of coffee or tea while we waited. Bravo! They even took our flight plan to the flight service station for filing and brought back weather information for us.

By 21:20 our wheels were in the well and we were back on course to Ciampino Airport, Rome.[16] We arrived at 01:10, which was good time for the 640-nautical-mile flight. The weather had turned bad about one hour south of Rome, and by the time we arrived, it was raining hard, and we were vectored for an ILS runway 15 Ciampino.

---

16. The route was direct Korinthos (KOR), R-19 Kerkira (KRK), A-14 Teano (TEA), then direct to Frosinone (FRS), and then direct Ciampino Airport, Rome, Italy.

21

Rome

Thursday, March 26, 1987

François Airault, from the organization staff, was waiting for us in Rome, and the paperwork was minimal. The Italians did not check our passports or our luggage. We left the terminal building and waited for the cab that François had called.

One cab pulled up, stopped, and we began to get in. The driver asked us if we had called a cab, and François said that we had. He said, in that case, that we could not ride with him, as he had not been called. We were about to argue the point, but just then another cab pulled up. We had the same conversation with the driver of this cab, during which time a third cab arrived. This also was not the cab we had called, so the drivers of the three cabs began an animated and sometimes angry discussion, accentuated on occasion by interjections from François and me.

I finally started talking about how tired I was, and said that I did not care who was called and who wasn't, but that I simply wanted somebody who drove a cab to take us to the hotel. The third driver then agreed to drive us.

On the drive to the hotel, we saw cobblestone streets that appeared to be remnants from the old Roman times but, unfortunately, not much more. Since we arrived late at night and were to leave early the next morning, we were deprived of experiencing the incredible buildings, monuments, and other beautiful treasures and interesting places to explore in Rome.

We were told that the day before, when we were having our airplane repaired in Cairo, the competitors had been driven from the hotel to the airport in vintage cars, with a police escort for a huge air show attended by 30,000 people. We were sorry to have missed this time in Rome.

We arrived at the hotel, the Joly Hotel, Via Veneto. When we walked into the lobby, all of the race participants, staff, and photographers who had evidently stayed up to greet us stood and applauded. They were well aware of all of the problems that we had experienced and were concerned about us. They also gave us an enormous bottle of champagne.

The hotel workers were on strike, so the organization had sent someone to a restaurant across the street and had a fine Italian meal brought to our room. They sent a dinner to Allen's room as well, but they had neglected to send food for François. However, our two meals were extremely large, and we shared with him. We had enough for the three of us with leftovers. We also shared a bottle or two of wine. It was 2:00 a.m. when François left and we went to bed.

Since the hotel staff was on strike, the next morning was total chaos. We finally paid what few charges we owed and departed on the bus for the airport at 07:00. Again, when Jim and I climbed aboard the bus, everyone applauded. It made us feel special.

22

Rome to Paris

It is sad that all things must come to an end. Even this international air race. We were nostalgic about it all as we prepared to leave on the last leg of our historic flight. We had become a family. In some ways—unrealistic ways—we would have liked to have the race adventure continue. But it was not to be.

On the morning of March 27, 1987, we arrived at Ciampino Airport early and saw the stands that had been set up for the air show the day before. We ate breakfast in a small trailer at the airport since the hotel workers were on strike, and we picked up our lunches to eat in the airplane during our flight to Paris.

Bernard Lamy and the rest of the technical team except for François Airault and Jean-Claude Kaufmann had taken off for Paris early, so the competitors were left to take off in order. François and Jean-Claude were the only members of the technical team left to assist if there were any problems.

Many of us needed fuel, and Jim and I were shocked when we received the fuel bill, as we were charged $5.50 per US gallon, which was expensive at that time. When Jim asked the man on the fuel truck why the charge was so high, he said, "It's because the United States is not a member of the Common Market." Wow! That was the most expensive fuel that we purchased during the entire race.

Everyone was anxious to get under way. We experienced one of the few foul-ups—at least in our opinion it was a foul-up—of the entire race at Ciampino. No one can fault an organization that performed flawlessly up to that point. First, all of the leaders—Bernard, Claude, and others—had climbed on board the organization aircraft and departed for Paris to prepare for our arrival there prior to the other airplanes' departures. This left one fellow from the organization to handle the departures.

We had each been assigned a departure time by Bernard during the previous evening. Jim and I were given the takeoff order and were number 9, right after the Cathay Pacific team. We had filed an IFR flight plan from Rome via Nice to Paris.

The Rome Ciampino controllers were not efficient, and this is definitely an understatement. There were many delays, and the Chronopost team was in position, holding for takeoff for over an hour before they were allowed to depart.

Several airplanes, including our own, had filed IFR flight plans because the weather was terrible in France. However, some of the other aircraft—it turned out most of the other aircraft—filed VFR flight plans on the theory that they would not have to depart in the assigned sequence. They did not have to wait for clearances and began taking off out of order, and thus those of us who were departing IFR had to wait even longer. This caused utter chaos and some hard feelings for a little while.

The aircraft that had filed IFR had to wait until their flight plans were processed in the computer, which took an eternity, while the VFR aircraft took off. This had never occurred on the entire trip and was really disconcerting.

I was on the radio for this leg, and at one point, I complained to Jean-Claude, who said there was nothing he could do about it, as the airplanes were entitled to take off VFR if they wished. That was not the way the organization usually did things. Finally, I got on the radio and told ground control that we wanted to taxi and take off. They knew we were in an air race. We were supposed to take off ninth, and already we were pushed back to fourteenth because other airplanes were taking off out of sequence.

The *Italia Wings* team also had requested start-up, but they were supposed to be behind us, and I told this to ground control. Ground control verified this with *Italia Wings,* who said that we were correct, and so we finally were allowed to taxi and take off. With all of the delays and foul-ups, we finally departed at 12:42.[17]

Italia Wings was in a good position to win the race, and afterward I felt bad insisting that we take off ahead of them. When I expressed this to Jim, he reminded me that their time would not start until they took off, so it would not hinder them. I was happy, as they were a nice crew who had become friends, and I would not want to do anything to impede their chances.

Initially, we flew at 8,000 feet, the flight level that we had requested. We had to fly low because of the blasted, ever-present headwinds. The flight was uneventful from Rome to the French coast, and then we entered the clouds.

At Nice, we turned north and headed to Paris. The route required a climb to 12,000 feet after Nice, and even though the safe altitude for that area was 12,000 feet and we were at 8,000 feet, the controller said that we could stay there if we wished to do so "at our own responsibility." This, to us, meant that if we could see the mountains and avoid them, we did not have to climb to 12,000 feet.

The clouds were intermittent, so even though many mountain peaks of the Alps were obscured, we could see those on our path. I wanted to fly lower to make better time since the winds, as usual, were worse the higher we climbed. Jim did not want any of that and said that we must fly by the book. This climb resulted in one of the few disagreements that we had during the entire race. Jim prevailed, simply because it was safer to fly the route as specified on the low level en route chart. In addition, I wanted to cut a corner instead of flying directly to a VOR and then turning like all of the other competitors had done throughout the race. Jim, also, would not do this.

---

17. Our route was direct to Ostia (OST), R-46 MEDAL, A-1 Elba (ELB), R-15 Montelimar (MTL), A-6 Dijon (DIG), B-37 Troyes (TRO), then direct to Coulommiers (CLM), for the VOR/DME runway 25 approach to Le Bourget Airport, Paris, France.

We finally did have some good tailwinds on this part of the trip and for a while were making good speed. However, as we neared Paris, we were in and out of the clouds and experienced rain and finally blowing snow. We never experienced icing, but we had a great deal of turbulence. The last hour of the race was one of the most turbulent, and we bounced along to Le Bourget Airport.

As we approached Paris, we were required to enter a holding pattern, and we had to circle around twice before we were permitted to land. The wind was blowing out of the west at about 40 knots. We had a tremendous crab angle and were blown still farther east than we would have liked.

After some delay, we were cleared for the approach. On this approach we saw Charles de Gaulle Airport before we saw Le Bourget. This caused us a few seconds confusion, duly noted by Patrick Seurat—a French controller with the organization—who always was present when we had the slightest problem. Because of the strong winds, the runway was changed by the tower to runway 21. We landed and taxied to the parking area. The time was 16:04.

The first thing we noticed was that we had beaten Chronopost to Paris. We had accomplished this, even though Chronopost left Rome before we did. Mama and Papa Chronopost were on the ground to welcome us, and we gave them the position of their airplane, which was not far behind.

Our children, Edward and Lisa, along with Stephanie Vasilovich and Jack Weisberg and Maryke, friends from Fresno, were there to meet us. We had expected Edward, Lisa, and Stephanie, but were surprised to see Jack and Maryke. They had been visiting Amsterdam and decided to fly down to welcome us.

We were happy to see everyone, but we were sad that the race was over. It was hard to believe that we had actually competed in and completed this air race of over 20,000 nautical miles between Paris and Beijing. When Jim first read the article from *Flying* magazine to me so long ago, we had no idea that this day would come. We were proud of what we had accomplished, even though sometimes we stumbled.

The European and Hong Kong teams were more worldly about international flying than we were—particularly those who were professional pilots, which most were. For example, almost all of their team members spoke English, which is the international language of the air, and frequently another language as well as their first language. The controllers along the route spoke to us in English, but it was often difficult to understand their English. The French and Italian teams seemed to understand them better than we did. We often had to ask the controllers to repeat their instructions by saying "Say again! Say again!"

Prior to our departure, we knew that this would be a historic flight. We had expectations that we might be compared to Charles and Amelia, but as it turned out, we were more likely to be compared to "wrong-way Corrigan."[18] We were naive, poorly prepared, and overconfident. But we had done it!

---

18 In 1938, Finn Corrigan flew from Long Beach, California, to New York City. He filed a flight plan for a return to California but instead flew to Ireland!

23

Paris

Friday, March 27, 1987

Edward, Lisa, and Stephanie had an adventure of their own coming to meet us. None of them had been out of the US before, so they were excited to be flying to Paris. They managed to find their hotel and then tried to figure out how to get to Le Bourget Airport. They took the Metro, but got off about 5 miles from where they were supposed to be. They hiked along the road, watching the airplanes land to see which direction they should go, and finally arrived, cold but sweaty from their long walk. They were excited to see the race airplanes land and watch the pilots get out and celebrate. There was so much happy energy!

They rushed to greet us and hug us when we landed. There was so much going on, it was difficult to take in everything that was happening, but everyone was excited and happy. Since it was extremely windy and cold at Le Bourget, we all went inside as soon as possible.

After a short time, Jim and I were taken to our hotel, the Holiday Inn République, where everyone was staying after the race. We immediately got a lot of ice and put it in the bidet, where the large bottle of champagne that we were given in Rome fit perfectly. After the champagne cooled, we had a celebratory toast, and Edward, Lisa, Stephanie, Jack, and Maryke returned

Our children, Edward and Lisa, greet us at Le Bourget
Airport on the final landing of the race.

to their respective hotels. We all needed to change clothes for the official end-of-the-race dinner.

Jack and Maryke fell asleep and never made it to the dinner. Edward, Lisa, and Stephanie got lost and were about an hour late, but they finally arrived and the party began. There was dancing after the dinner, and Bernard presented an armful of flowers to the women pilots. I received mine in the middle of the dance floor.

The competitors were asked to vote for their favorite crew, and as the ballots were being passed out,

Jim with our celebratory
champagne that had been
chilled in the bidet.

the TDK team passed out TDK pens, obviously looking for votes. Everyone was in a festive mood, celebrating the successful completion of this historic air race.

Saturday, March 28, 1987

The buses picked us up at the hotel for the final awards ceremony and luncheon at Mirapolis, an amusement park that was being built by Dr. Ghaith Pharaon outside of Paris. There was a huge statue of Gargantua at the entry to the park, and strangely it was necessary to walk through his crotch to enter.

The ceremony and luncheon were held in a huge yellow tent with red stripes that had a stage in the middle, bleachers on one side, and linen-covered, formally set tables at the other side. There were a lively band, jugglers, acrobats, cyclists, and a myriad of other entertainers to keep up our spirits. There were, as usual, a few speeches—one by the head of the French Aeronautical Association—and, of course, the final one by Bernard.

Italia Wings won the first-place trophy for the Beijing-to-Paris portion of the race. *Manpower* won second place, and *Microjet-Mammouth* came in third. The Cathay Pacific team, *Spirit of Hong Kong*, won the safety award. The favorite crew was announced—the one voted by the other crews the evening before as being the favorite—and Jim and I won this award, which was presented by Fabio Isman of *Il Messaggero.* We had come in last in the race, due to our extra day delay in Cairo, but this award pleased us more than first place would have.

The dinner was delicious, as is to be expected in France, but then it was time to say goodbye, and everyone was hugging, kissing, and crying. I was doing well until I had to say goodbye to Reza. Perhaps it was because the other competitors have homes, and theoretically we would be able to visit them or they us in the future. Reza seemed to be generally without one, or at least one that we knew of. As an international photographer, he traveled from place to place, ordinarily to the hot spots of the world, so I felt that we might not see him again. Also, he had been La Girafe's best friend on the trip, and somewhat closer to us than some of the others.

Statue of Gargantua at the entrance to Mirapolis.

In general, the goodbyes were a blur. I do recall that Patricia, whom I had come to know better as the race went on, seemed particularly affected. She hugged me and hung on, not wanting to let go. And as I hugged her back, tears again came to my eyes, as I didn't want to let go either. I could hardly manage a brief goodbye to Bernard, who had made this all possible and never did say goodbye to Maryse at all that day, which I regretted as she had worked hard throughout the race to make the activities during our stops go smoothly, and I did not know whether we would ever see her again.

Winning the race was never important to us. We had shared the experience of a lifetime and learned so much about flying and the world. We had made friends from all over the world, some of whom remain good, close, and valued friends. We proved to ourselves that we could meet whatever challenges that arose.

On Saturday evening after we returned from dinner, there was a message waiting for us that a good friend from Fresno, Edna Smith, had called. She was in town, as were Joan and Rosa, our friends from Barcelona. It

Our children, Lisa and Edward, with Christian
Rosenquist on the Eiffel Tower.

was too late to call that night, so I called Edna the next morning. She said that she had come to meet us but thought we were coming a day later than we actually did. She said that Joan and Rosa had come from Barcelona to see us as well.

I told Edna that we had plans to leave for Aubigny and Royan with some of the other competitors that day and would probably not be back until sometime on Monday morning. She thought that Joan and Rosa would have to leave on Monday. We were disappointed, but there was nothing we could do.

Edward and Lisa had become friends with the Rosenquists' children, Christian and Gretchen. They toured Paris together and hung out for a while with Reza at the hotel. They walked all over Paris and took the stairs to the top of the Eiffel Tower. It was an exciting time, romantic for all of them, and they enjoyed the moment. Christian kissed Lisa at the top of the Eiffel Tower, which made it even more memorable.

They were all invited to go with Bruno, Didier, and Patricia Lamy and their dates to a disco, Les Bains. This was the hot spot in Paris, with an expensive cover charge and dinner. Bruno and Didier evidently paid the tab. Yannick Noah, the great tennis player, was the only recognizable celebrity present. They danced until 4:00 or 4:30 a.m., and then they all crashed in Gretchen's room. Lisa reported that Bruno and Didier were awesome dancers.

24

Post-Race: Aubigny/Royan

Sunday, March 29, 1987

Before returning to Paris, we had been invited by François and Maurice to fly to Aubigny-sur-Nère, the home of the *Bio-France Elevage* team, for a small reception and lunch welcoming them home. Jean-Michel Masson also would be there, and he invited us to attend a reception that was to be held for him afterward in Royan, on the Atlantic Coast. Since we were reluctant to say goodbye to all of our new friends, we decided to attend both.

On Sunday morning, March 29, we went to the airport with Gaston, the French controller and member of the race organization and who had picked up the money from me at the hotel before the race. We had agreed to fly Gaston to Royan. We checked the weather, which was not great but better than much of what we had experienced many times during the last month. It appeared to be acceptable, and we decided to fly VFR, low and under the clouds.

Jean-Michel Masson and his girlfriend, Françoise, flying in his Trinidad, and Jim and I, in our Cessna 210 with Gaston, left Le Bourget with a first stop at Aubigny. Allen was still suffering from a bad cold, so he stayed in the hotel in Paris.

It was snowing when we took off from Le Bourget. We climbed to 1,300 feet and executed the published VFR departure (southbound) en route to Aubigny. We laughed about flying "French VFR," which meant in and out of clouds. Gaston handled the radios. After less than one hour, we entered the pattern to land.

We landed at Aubigny on a grass strip soon after Jean-Michel had landed. We were concerned about mud and getting stuck, but were assured that the field was fine, which it was. François and Maurice were there to greet us, along with the president of the local aéroclub.

Upon landing, we were introduced to the mayor, the president of the Aubigny Flying Club, and other dignitaries. Our three airplanes were lined up for photographs. Our hosts were François Dabin, the pilot of the *Bio-France Elevage*, and photojournalist Maurice Painchaud. The other crew member, copilot Gilles Rousseau, a French controller, was unable to make the trip.

After we looked at the Aubigny Flying Club's airplanes and facilities, we were driven through Aubigny. It is a beautiful, old city that has retained many of its early buildings, some of which are 200 years old.

We were then taken to the farm of *Bio-France Elevage's* principal sponsor, or at least to his land. It was raining a little, and now and again, it snowed. The roadway into the farm was muddy. We drove through the property, and at one point came upon a double gate. We left our cars outside and entered on foot but hesitated when we were advised that a boar hunt was in progress. Having visions of California wild boars, we were not about to set foot in the middle of an area where one was running about and being chased by a pack of dogs. We could hear the hounds in hot pursuit of the boar.

François went on ahead and soon beckoned to us that it was safe to progress and not to worry. We walked farther, following François on foot up a muddy road toward all of the racket. Soon we were introduced to a friendly farmer (the sponsor), his wife, and other family members. We asked about the boar hunt.

He said, "Soon you will see him," and shortly thereafter, we did see an enormous black boar. He was loping along across the field at a rather comfortable gait, not running fast, followed by a pack of hounds, howling and barking loudly but making no real effort to catch or corner the boar. They all disappeared again into the forest.

The farmer explained to us that the boar was to be caught by men, not the dogs, and then put into a cage, fed, and allowed to rest. In a week or two he would be allowed to escape again, and they would have another boar hunt, with the same result. Evidently, both the boar and the dogs were in on this game and did not take it too seriously. How civilized!

We left the hunting grounds and returned to a small hotel/restaurant/bar in Aubigny for lunch, which was served in a large back room where a table was laid out and waiting for us. We have always thought that the French have forgotten more about food than we in the United States will ever know. The proprietors served us a six-course gourmet French meal, which was one of the best we had in France.

The beverages began with kir, then four types of wine, ending with an excellent coffee. There were several courses, including a delicious boar pâté (how did this happen?). I had *ris de veau* (sweetbreads) for my main course and Jim had duck. Profiteroles were served for dessert. Everything was excellent.

After the meal, we adjourned to the laundry room, which doubled as an exercise and TV room, to watch a fifty-minute television program about the air race. French television, and evidently a lot of French people, had been tracking our progress with weekly specials.

After the meal and after watching the TV program about the race, we returned to the airport. More people had arrived to catch a glimpse of the crazy pilots and their airplanes. We had begun to prepare our Cessna and Jean-Michel's Trinidad for the flight to Royan, when we all were asked to return to the clubhouse and wait because the mayor would be arriving shortly with the champagne.

He arrived, and French champagne was brought out and served in crystal flutes. No plastic for the French! We were moved. Jim said that in the US we had a rule—"eight hours between the bottle and the throttle." They were astounded, and we were advised that the French would never be able to fly if they adhered to the American rule. They joked that it could be amended to provide "eight meters between the bottle and the throttle" or, in the alternative, "eight minutes between the bottle and the throttle."

Jim proposed a toast to French-American friendship that was quite lengthy because he had to remember to include all of the dignitaries who were present. He then took a polite sip of the champagne, since he would be flying. I downed my glass, since I was not. We then departed for Royan, after first embracing our friends, François and Maurice, whom we could not soon forget.

From Aubigny, we flew west over the beautiful French countryside to Royan. Jean-Michel flew his Trinidad beside our airplane. Gaston hailed from this region of France and pointed out the various points of interest. He showed us the airfield where he learned to fly and the little town where he was born. On reaching the coast, we flew over the beach, and Gaston pointed out the nude beach area below. There were no bathers that day, since it was near freezing. It had snowed in Aubigny while we were having lunch.

After perhaps an hour, in improving weather—though the wind was blowing at about 30 to 40 knots out of the west and it was quite cold—we arrived in Royan. Royan is situated on the Atlantic Coast at the south of the estuary leading to the Bordeaux region to the south. Gaston said that it was destroyed during World War II. Later, we saw pictures of the heavy fighting in the area, including one spectacular picture of twin-engine American bombers making a bombing run on Royan from the sea while under heavy enemy fire.

We landed in Royan and were greeted by the mayor and a number of the townspeople who had prepared another reception. Jean-Michel was treated like a conquering hero. For many years, he had a summer home in Royan, and he still hangared and maintained his airplane there. Again, there was a reception with much food and drink. The mayor made a special effort to assure that Jim and I were not left out.

The people were friendly, and, as in Aubigny, they all had their pictures taken with us by the airplane. One of the people called a member of the aéroclub who had not come to greet us and who was married to an American woman. She did not arrive, but her husband and his twin brother did. They were both gorgeous, had deep blue eyes, and had formerly been models. We were told later that the American wife was the daughter of the president of Citibank. They resided either in New York or Royan, occasionally traveling to the Orient or wherever they wished.

Gaston loaned me his sweater, as it was extremely cold, and then he left, promising to see us in the morning, as he intended to fly back to Paris with us. Jean-Michel had brought his girlfriend, Françoise, with him.

Notwithstanding the French rule about eight meters between the bottle and throttle, we opted to stay overnight in Royan and went to the hotel to drop off our luggage. Jean-Michel and Françoise also stayed for the night. Jean-Michel invited his airplane mechanic and his wife to join us for dinner.

We dined at an attractive restaurant overlooking the harbor and the food was great. It was one of the more unusual dinners, in that the mechanic and his wife did not speak English. Therefore, Jean-Michel translated between English and French. Françoise was talking little and smoking a lot. The mechanic sat next to me, and his wife sat across the table from him, next to Jean-Michel, chatting pleasantly.

Monday, March 30, 1987

The next morning, we left Royan early and Jean-Michel accompanied us to the airport. Gaston never came to the airport and did not return to Paris with us. Jean-Michel told us that prior to the beginning of the race, Gaston had been involved in a car accident. He had been drinking and struck a little boy crossing the street, who had subsequently died. Jean-Michel thought it was quite probable that Gaston would have to go to prison. Gaston had always appeared happy, smiling, and full of fun during the trip. One would never have guessed that he was carrying this heavy burden.

Jean-Michel called Paris for the weather and scurried around to find the appropriate charts. Gaston, who was supposed to accompany us back to Paris, had elected to stay for a while in Royan. This created a bit of a problem because the tower controller did not speak English. Jim checked the oil as part of the preflight and discovered that it was one quart low. The flight instructor for the Royan Flying Club arrived at about the same time and, in a gesture consistent with our good treatment throughout France, found a liter of oil to put in the airplane and a spare, which he gave to us. He refused to be paid for the oil.

We had gone up in the tower with Jean-Michel and knew that the tower operators did not speak English, so when Jim called the tower for taxi instructions, the reply was simply "two nine." We taxied to the end of runway 29, completed the warmup, and, after looking around for other traffic, reported that we were prepared to depart. The controllers simply again said "two nine" and nothing more. We assumed that we had been cleared for takeoff and lifted off, heading toward Paris.

On the way, we flew over the Loire Valley. The fellow who had given us the oil also gave us a chart with the Loire Valley chateaus marked on it. He had circled the chateaus and let us keep the chart. We flew over Chenonceau, which is particularly stunning, since it is built across the river Cher. We did a 360-degree turn over the chateau to get a better view. We next flew to Chaumont, on the Loire, a smaller chateau that is set back somewhat from the river. The third chateau was Chambord, which is probably the most beautiful of all the chateaus, and the most interesting from the air. It truly looked like a fairytale palace.

The weather began to worsen, and by the time we arrived in Paris it was snowing again, and we were flying "French VFR." We called Le Bourget and made the VFR approach from the west at 1,300 feet. We taxied the airplane over to the maintenance hangar, and I waited by the airplane while Jim went inside to talk to the mechanic. As he returned to the airplane, we saw the organization airplane, *Gulf Echo Papa Yankee*, being towed in, obviously also for maintenance.

Tuesday, March 31, 1987

Claudine Sobol-Oosterlinck picked me up to go shopping. We first went to a lingerie store, as I had promised our daughter-in-law, Connie, that I would buy her a nightgown in Paris. The nightgown/robe sets were about $1,500. They were pure silk and beautiful, but this was more than I wanted to spend. I finally settled for a nightgown alone, which was on sale for $200. Claudine pointed out that the VAT tax would be refunded if it was being taken out of the country. We went to various other shops, but the prices were outrageous. Most of the items were more than they would have been at home. I did, however, buy one dress for myself and a couple of shirts for Jim.

Claudine and I met Jim and Claudine's husband for lunch.

That evening, the Association of Women Pilots in Paris held a reception for Claudine, and she invited me to go with her. It was held in a small suite of offices on the third floor of a rather nice old building. Afterward, one of the women drove me to the restaurant, Auberge des Deux Cygnes, where Jim, the kids, and Edna Smith, our friend from Fresno, were waiting. The restaurant was fantastic—small but nice. There was an old well along one side of the restaurant, which evidently had some historical significance. There was also a beautiful stained-glass window on one wall.

Wednesday, April 1, 1987

Our daughter Lisa and I went shopping in all of the designer stores including Christian Dior and Valentino. We bought nothing, since the prices were extremely high, but we enjoyed looking. We were both depressed, knowing that it was our last day in Paris, but the weather was beautiful, the sun was shining, and we tried to forget that we were leaving.

I asked her how she felt about us flying this race, and she said that she was never frightened for us and always assumed that we would be safe. To her, our adventure was exciting and interesting, and it was what we should do. She assumed that we could take care of any situation that arose and admitted that she was perhaps as naive as we were. She only thought about how interesting and exciting it would be. When we returned home, our daughter Karen expressed much the same feeling.

We took a commercial flight. Our airplane left at 5:00 p.m., so we left the hotel at approximately 2:00. Allen had returned to stay at the Crillon, and we had not seen him since our return to Paris. Edward, Lisa, and Stephanie took the Metro from their hotel, so Jim and I simply met everyone at the airport. It did not take long to check in, so we had lunch in the airport restaurant and then looked at the items in the duty-free shop. Surprisingly, these were also expensive, so we bought nothing.

Although Jim and I had purchased the least expensive, tourist class tickets for the airplane ride home, our seats were changed, and we were shown to the upper deck of the 747. This is a small, more exclusive, totally nonsmoking area. Evidently Bernard or someone from the race had called and obtained the upgrade for us. Bernard had asked the time of our flight, so we suspect that it was he. The kids remained in tourist class, which was extremely crowded with many children and small babies.

Since we were traveling westward, we followed the sun and arrived in Los Angeles at 6:30 p.m. We both dozed during the flight, but did not sleep much, as we had on the flight to Paris. In Los Angeles, we caught the Delta Airlines flight to Fresno. Jim, Allen, Edward, Lisa, Stephanie, and I arrived in Fresno on the same day we left Paris, April 1, 1987. Our son Kevin was there to meet us, as was Stephanie's family. At first, it felt like another stopover on the air race, but after a short time, we realized that we did not have to refuel or file flight plans.

As we taxied in, Jim and I reminisced. Our touchdown at Le Bourget was the last of the air race. This touchdown in Fresno would be the end of our adventure. No more all-night flights through bad weather. No more heavily armed men escorting me to the *toilette* or the bank. No more daily parties or events. No more spending time with our race family. We were leaving the unique world that we had inhabited for over a month for the familiar world of home. We made memories that we will never forget and met challenges that we never anticipated. We made it. We knew we could do it, and we did it. We hugged.

We were home and happy to be there safe and sound. The first night in our own bed was wonderful. We had a real *toilette* and could depend on having toilet paper. It took us a few days to adjust.

JIM'S NOTES: *When we began planning to fly the Paris-Pékin-Paris air race, Judy and I were only acquainted with the geography of the part of the earth that we were going to overfly from books and television. Our flight revealed that the earth is vastly more beautiful and varied than we could have imagined.*

We were impressed by the friendliness that we experienced from the people everywhere. There are many examples, but we remember specifically the helpful mechanics and staff in Dhaka, Bangladesh, and Cairo who refused to accept any compensation for their tremendous and competent work.

The race organization staff and other competitors were friendly and helpful, and we will always remember the unique times we shared. Perhaps this race is further evidence that humans have the ability and fortitude to compete in such a challenging and demanding adventure. It was our great pleasure to participate in this unusual, difficult, beautiful, and memorable adventure. The memories will always be precious to us.

25

Post-Race: Fresno

Our airplane had remained in Paris for some needed maintenance. Dick Smith returned to Paris to fly it back to California. This time he had great weather, VFR all the way, and made the whole trip in three days without incident.

RECEPTIONS

To celebrate our homecoming, the Friends of the Fresno Airport held a big reception for us in a hangar at Executive Wings, the FBO at the airport where we kept our airplane. Even though our airplane already had arrived, Jim and I took off and flew it in again for the reception and the ever-present TV cameras.

This was the first of many receptions and speaking engagements. The media coverage seemed to be nonstop. All of the TV stations and the *Fresno Bee* (the local newspaper) had extensive coverage of us during the race, and both Jim and I were interviewed many times after our return to Fresno.

The Fresno County Bar Association bulletin published a three-page article about our flight. The following year, on February 17, 1988, I was the keynote speaker for a high school math and science conference (about 4,000 students) held at Fresno City College. It felt great to be able to

We may have had a dragon on our tail, but also had La Girafe along for the ride. "George" poses with our airplane.

inspire the young people, and I subsequently was asked to speak at various schools and career-day events.

The Fresno chapter of the Ninety-Nines, the international women pilots' association that Mohini Shroff belonged to in Bombay, invited me to speak, and I became a member as I promised Mohini I would.

VALLEY CHILDREN'S HOSPITAL AND LA GIRAFE

We returned La Girafe to Valley Children's Hospital. We were sad, as he had become a part of our crew and our life, but he belonged to them and they had only loaned him to us for the flight.

On April 28, we received a telephone call from Valley Children's Hospital informing us that they had received a letter and a check—a donation from King Hussein of Jordan in the amount of $10,000. They were excited, and so were we. They held a small reception to celebrate, and in addition to thanking us, they gave us the giraffe to keep. We were thrilled to have him back.

At that time, they told us that his name was George. We never knew that, and he will always be La Girafe to us. The hospital also published a wonderful article about us, the giraffe, and the race.

KEEPING IN TOUCH

We kept in touch with many of the people from the air race. We returned to France almost every year, and I celebrated my fiftieth birthday in Paris with a dinner hosted by Bernard and Maryse. Many of the pilots attended, as did Reza, the race photographer. He had to leave early, as Nelson Mandela was being released from prison in South Africa and he was to be there to capture the moment.

In 1988, Lisa spent six months in Europe, and we met her in Paris for her twenty-fourth birthday. The previous evening, Bernard and Maryse had arranged a beautiful dinner for her on a boat on the Seine. Since her birthday is July 14, Bastille Day, a band was rehearsing *La Marseillaise*. Bernard said it was just for her.

We visited Bernard and Maryse many times, and they also came to Fresno to visit us. On one of our trips to France, Bernard rented a small airplane and flew us to Normandy. We had never been there, and he flew low, about 50 feet over the beaches made famous in the D-Day invasion.

We then landed and he gave us a tour of the historic sites, including the cemetery. He told us that when his children were young, he had brought them there and told them, "This is what the Americans did for us!" It was emotional, and while we were there, an elderly man, obviously American, walked among the tombstones to one that he recognized. Through tears, he told us that this was his buddy who was killed on D-Day, and this was the first time he had returned to honor him.

We attended Bernard's seventieth birthday in 2000 and were the only Americans among his friends from many countries who attended. Sadly, we were also the only Americans who attended his funeral in September 2006. We had long ago become family.

THE ROYAL PALACE

AMMAN   JORDAN

25 April, 1987

Dear Sir,

   During the Paris-Beijing Air Race the participants
made a stop-over in Jordan at which time His Majesty
King Hussein I met with them all, and learnt of the fund-
raising efforts of Jim Bell and Judy Bell.

   It is, therefore, with much pleasure that I enclose
a cheque in the sum of US$ 10,000 as a personal donation
from His Majesty The King to the Valley Children's Hospital
Foundation.

                     Yours sincerely,

                     Marwan S. Kasim
                     Chief of the Royal Hashemite Court

Valley Children's Hospital Foundation
3151 N. Millbrook
Fresno
CA 93703
United States of America

Letter to Valley Children's Hospital with donation from King Hussein.

We also kept in touch with Bernard's children: Patricia, Didier, and Bruno. Bruno's son, David, came to live with us in Fresno for a month so that he could fly and build hours in order to be hired by an airline. He is now a captain with Air France, as is his father. He is our French grandson, and he considers us his American grandparents.

In 2018, Bruno was the captain of the Air France A-380 on which we were flying to Paris. He allowed us to sit with him on the flight deck. We did not expect to be acquainted with the pilot on the return flight, so when it was announced that François Garçon (from the TDK team) was the captain, we asked the flight attendant to take a note to him asking whether he had flown the '87 Paris-Pékin-Paris Air Race.

Within minutes, he was at our side, hugging, kissing, and greeting us. Of course, he invited us to the flight deck as well. What a wonderful surprise.

David Beechcroft-Kay of the Hong Kong team visited us with his wife, Terry, many times, and we visited them in Hong Kong. One year we flew to Hong Kong for David's birthday. He was the captain on our Cathay Pacific Airlines flight and invited us to the flight deck to witness the descent into Hong Kong.

When he retired, they moved to Mougins in southern France, and we visited them there many times as well. David's oldest son, Steven, also lived with us in Fresno for a month. David had rented a small airplane, and Steven flew it for hours each day to build up his flying time, as it was much less expensive to fly here than in France or England. Steven, our British grandson, is now a captain with British Air.

We became good friends with Gérard Emler and his wife, Marie, and visited with them in France nearly every year. They joined us in Marrakesh, along with our children and David and Terry, to celebrate the millennium at the end of 1999. We look to Gérard as our expert for advice on restaurants, wines, and great places to stay. Sadly, Marie passed away a few years ago.

We visited with Gilles Rousseau and Nicole, his wife, both in France and in Fresno. On one occasion, they were our guides for a trip to the Brittany region where Nicole was from.

We also exchanged many visits with Jean-Michel Masson and Jean Le Ber together, separately, with, and without their spouse and/or significant others. Each had married after the race. Jean gave us an inside tour of the European Space Agency. Jean-Michel guided us around Tours and the Loire Valley, and then he moved to Royan, where we visit him now.

Mauro Masson, captain of *Italia Wings*, became a great and valued friend, and we see him almost every year, either here in the US or in Italy. One year we met for lunch in Cuba—unplanned, but a pleasant surprise. He brought his children to our home when they were young, and we took them to Columbia, an Old West town, where they rode a stagecoach. On another occasion, we vacationed with Mauro and Elizabetta in Sicily. We feel as though they are family also.

We visited with Tim Knatchbull in London in March 2015, and he gave us a copy of the book he had written, *From a Clear Blue Sky: Surviving the Mountbatten Bomb*. It is an emotional and moving story.

We learned a few years ago that Gaston, the air traffic controller who flew with us to Royan, was killed when he was hit by a car crossing the street.

We kept in touch with the Rosenquists for many years, visiting them at their home in Napa. Gretchen, their daughter, had married Alain Théveneau, the photojournalist from the TDK team, and they moved to Corsica and then Mauritius. In the beginning, Gretchen didn't speak French and Alain did not speak much English, but they each learned quickly— Gretchen by watching French TV.

Patricia, Bernard's daughter, subsequently married François Airault, who had been so helpful to us in Rome. She became a balloonist and on one occasion when we stayed with them, she took me up in a balloon early in the morning, over the French countryside. She subsequently bought a "balloon farm" north of Bordeaux, where balloons can land and which is occasionally the starting point for balloon races.

There were other romantic stories from the air race, but for privacy reasons, we will let them remain untold.

RELEVANT HISTORICAL EVENTS

In 1989, the pro-democracy movement in the People's Republic of China resulted in protests in Tian'anmen Square. They were forcibly suppressed when the government declared martial law and sent tanks into the square, resulting in many deaths. We wondered whether the Minister of

Public Security who sat at our table for the official dinner, toasted Jim, and had been so friendly was responsible.

On February 7, 1999, King Hussein's eldest son, Crown Prince Abdullah II bin Al-Hussein (Prince Abdullah, as I knew him) became King on the death of his father. It seemed strange to see this nice young boy, now a man, take his place as the respected leader of this great country. We wondered if he was still flying and suspect that he does whenever he can.

1992 'ROUND THE WORLD AIR RACE

A few years after the historic Paris-Pékin-Paris Air Race, Bernard decided to organize the 1992 First 'Round the World Air Race beginning in Geneva and flying over Russia. Certainly we would not be crazy enough to contemplate doing this—right?

Bernard and Maryse had come to visit us in Fresno and were trying to decide on an appropriate race stop in the western United States after the airplanes had crossed Russia. They were contemplating somewhere in the San Francisco area, but were meeting with reluctance from the "powers that be" because of high traffic in the area.

Of course, Jim and I suggested Fresno, as we knew the people at the airport and maintenance facilities, and we could help plan parties and other events, such as a trip to nearby Yosemite National Park for the participants. They liked that idea and agreed. We arranged a meeting with the mayor and others who were encouraging and helpful, and Fresno became one of the stops (along with Washington, DC) in the United States.

Jim and I thought that if we would fly this race—and we really should not—we should do so in a twin-engine airplane. Jim already had his twin-engine rating, so I did the training and obtained mine—it was a necessary step, just in case. We had the opportunity to purchase a Cessna 421C "Golden Eagle," which was larger and more comfortable than the small Cessna 210 that we had flown to China. It even had a *toilette*.

Well, why not? It was just another small step.

Flight Terms

AIRWAY: An airway on an aviation chart is like a highway on a road map. Airways are identified by a letter and number. For example, A-99.

ADF: Automatic Direction Finder. Aircraft instrument showing the aircraft's position relative to the NDB station.

FBO: Fixed Base Operation. Place at an airport for the sale of fuel and other aviation-related products and maintenance of aircraft.

GLIDESLOPE: Part of the ILS system in the aircraft that governs the descent to the runway.

IFR: Instrument Flight Rules. Applies for flights in the clouds and all flights above 18,000 feet.

ILS: Instrument Landing System. Permits a pilot to land in inclement weather.

LOCALIZER: Part of the ILS system in the aircraft that matches the aircraft with the centerline of the runway.

NDB: Non-Directional Beacon. The ground station for the navigational system. An airplane flies to/from the NDB using the ADF.

SID: Standard Instrument Departure. The published departure procedure for aircraft departing in inclement weather.

TIME: A twenty-four-hour clock is used in aviation.

VFR: Visual Flight Rules. Applies to flights under 18,000 feet and clear of clouds.

VOR: Very High Frequency Omnidirectional Range. A ground station that emits a signal enabling an aircraft to fly to/from the station.

Air Race Organization Personnel

Bernard Lamy, the race director, had a passion, a love, a vision, and a dream: flying. For those of us who knew and loved him, he gave us a great gift—the adventure of a lifetime, friendships that will last forever, and unparalleled memories.

Bernard formulated the idea for the Paris-Pékin-Paris Air Race with Gérard Emler in 1985. He worked on it tirelessly—planning routes; organizing hotels, meals, press conferences, and activities at the mandatory stops; obtaining permission to overfly various countries; and overcoming incredible obstacles of every imaginable kind. His wonderful wife, Maryse, shared his passion and worked with him in every venue, making all the detailed arrangements that were necessary to house, feed, and entertain everyone. Their three children, Patricia, Didier, and Bruno, were active participants in the smooth running of the race and events.

His passion for aviation came early in life, as his grandfather was an administrator for Aéropostale that established air routes from France over the South Atlantic to South America. His organization, Arc en Ciel, was named after Jean Mermoz's airplane, the first to make this crossing. These routes were established after World War I and continued in operation until the beginning of World War II. Bernard was greatly influenced by the glamour and adventure that he imagined the French pilots experienced flying these routes. He was fascinated by airplanes and flying, and, of course, he became a pilot himself.

As a young man, he joined the French Air Force and, along with two other French pilots, attended cadet training at Hondo Air Base in Texas. After leaving the Air Force, he took a job flying throughout the Middle East selling pots and pans for Tefal, a cookware company.

Bernard flew as a competitor in the Air Transat air race from Paris to New York and back to Paris, caught the "air race fever," and began organizing air races himself. He began with microlight air races: London to Paris in 1982 and a Tour de France in 1983. After that, he organized the Transafricaine in 1983, which took the competitors from Paris to Libreville, Gabon and Marrakesh, Morocco and, in 1985, the route of the Courrier Sud, which followed the Aéropostale mail route from Toulouse to Rio de Janeiro and back to Toulouse. Then came the Paris-Pékin-Paris Air Race.

To top this, in 1992, he organized the First 'Round the World Air Race beginning in Geneva, Switzerland, crossing all of Russia and the United States before returning to Europe.

In his numerous press conferences, he often referred to the pilots who flew his air races as "Crazy But Not Stupid." That we were!

Maryse Lamy, Bernard's wife, planned and implemented the activities at the mandatory stops, including hotel stays and the many parties, dinners, and other activities in which we participated. She mainly managed all the financial part of the races.

Patricia Lamy, Bernard and Maryse's daughter, was in charge of communications and public relations. She is a balloonist and returned to China to fly over the Great Wall with her balloon in 2007. She now owns a "balloon farm."

Didier Lamy and Bruno Lamy, Bernard and Maryse's two sons, not only flew the second organization's Beechcraft 200 to carry the press, they also assisted at the various stops with refueling and other activities. They are both Air France captains.

Jean-Claude Kaufmann was a Swiss pilot who flew the organization's Falcon 20.

Reza, the official race photographer, is world renowned. He is an independent photographer whose photographs have appeared in most international publications, including *Life* magazine and *National Geographic*. He photographed the rise to power of Corazon Aquino in the Philippines in the 1980s and Benazir Bhutto's wedding. He spent several years in Afghanistan and traveled with Massoud, the head of the Northern Alliance. An incredibly interesting person.

Hubert Rault, the race mechanic, could fix anything, and he was much in demand through the race.

François Airault, Patrick Seurat, Jean Leygnac, and **Philippe Blouin (Gaston)** assisted with air traffic control in the control towers at various stops. François and Jean also helped with arrangements on the ground.

Claude and **Martine Jaubert** assisted Maryse with the hotels and other arrangements.

There were many other people who comprised the organization, most of whom we would recognize, but we do not have their names. They worked while we flew!

Race Sponsors

GÉRARD EMLER met Bernard Lamy in 1985 in Saint-Louis du Sénégal, at the end of the Courrier Sud air race, and because he shared Bernard's love and passion for aviation, joined him in planning and implementing the Paris-Pékin-Paris Air Race. He also became a main sponsor of the race. Gérard was present at most of the stops and participated in many of the press conferences.

Gérard's interest in flying probably began at birth. He is the son of one of those iconic pilots of Aéropostale, who flew the mail route from Toulouse, France, across the South Atlantic to Natal, Brazil, in the late 1920s and early 1930s. His father flew the Port-Etienne/Saint-Louis du Sénégal portion of this famous journey.

IL MESSAGGERO is one of the oldest Italian daily newspapers. It not only sponsored the race and covered it extensively, it also organized and sponsored an Aviation Day at the Ciampino airfield. Fabio Isman, representing *Il Messaggero*, presented a trophy to *Italia Wings* for winning the Amman-Rome leg of the race and then, at the final banquet, presented *Italia Wings* the trophy for winning the Beijing-Paris portion of the race.

INTERNIKE is linked with the Italian company Nicols Group, international insurance brokers.

PILAR is a Swiss branch of the Pilar Group, an international affairs bank that carries out market studies of high technology and pharmaceutical products and real estate development.

JEPPESEN is the world leader in flight information services and supplies. It gave each crew a binder with complete aeronautical documentation covering the entire itinerary of the race.

SARSAT-COSPAS is a company with a program that aids in search-and-rescue operations through detection and the ability to pinpoint a distress beacon. Sarsat beacons were given to each crew participating in the race.

GROUPE PHARAON was one of the major sponsors. Dr. Ghaith Pharaon was present at most of the mandatory stops and participated in some of the press conferences. He was educated in private schools in France, then Beirut, Lebanon, Syria, Switzerland, the Colorado School of Mines, Stanford University, and Harvard Business School (where he was a classmate of George Bush). After graduating from Harvard, Dr. Pharaon formed the Saudi Research and Development Corporation Ltd. (REDEC).

Ghaith's father, Rashed Pharaon, was the advisor to the Saudi monarchy for many years, as well as being the first Saudi Arabian ambassador to France.

The Competitors

Each team included the pilot, copilot, and photojournalist or reporter. Sometimes the team members were different for the outgoing leg, Paris to Beijing, from those on the inbound leg, Beijing to Paris. One airplane, the *Vail Snail,* included passengers as well. The tail numbers (following the name of the airplane) identify each airplane. The initial letter identifies the country in which the airplane is registered. Tail numbers of airplanes from the United States begin with N, those from France begin with F, from Italy I, from Belgium OO, and from Switzerland HB.

AAAAA-RENT-A-SPACE – N6798X

This Cessna 421C, "Golden Eagle," was the largest aircraft competing in the race. It carried extra fuel tanks for its twin engines, which gave it an endurance of nine and a half hours of flying time. The airplane was sponsored by AAAAA-Rent-A-Space, a ministorage facility owned by Jim Knuppe of San Francisco.

JAMES KNUPPE attached four gold stripes to his jacket and wore a cap trimmed with gold. As owner and sponsor of the aircraft, he was the aircraft's commander. He liked to describe himself as a self-made man, and he was deeply religious. According to his crew, he prayed prior to every takeoff—as it turned out, sometimes with good reason.

STEVE PICATTI, the copilot, also was from San Francisco, but after the race, he relocated to Oregon. He was a professional pilot, an aerobatics pilot, and a restorer of vintage aircraft.

MARC MOSIER was French but moved to New York and became the director of Banque Populaire. He was the representative of the Aéroclub de France in the US and a flight instructor. He subsequently left banking, moved to Virginia, and became an airplane broker, selling and ferrying aircraft all over North and South America, Europe, and Africa. His sense of humor was unparalleled, and he could imitate various accents perfectly. He was our initial contact for the race.

BIO-FRANCE ELEVAGE – F-GENS

This TB 20 Trinidad is a single-engine airplane with eight hours of fuel. The team, from Aubigny-sur-Nère, was sponsored by the Institut National de la Recherche Agronomique (I.N.R.A.), Credit Agricole, the Institute Mérieux (artificial insemination), and Chevillot (animalist marking). They carried with them a container of frozen animal semen for experiments in artificial insemination of Chinese cows. They had never flown outside of France, so this was a true adventure for them.

FRANÇOIS DABIN was the aircraft commander. He was the technical director of a company and the chief pilot and instructor of the Aubigny-sur-Nère aéroclub in Cher.

GILLES ROUSSEAU, the copilot, was an air traffic controller as well as a pilot.

MAURICE PAINCHAUD was the librarian of Aubigny-sur-Nère and a correspondent of the *Nouvelle République du Centre Ouest*.

CAFFÈ LAVAZZA – I-MEPY

The PA60 Aerostar twin-engine aircraft was the fastest of all the airplanes and was bought specially for the race. The problem was that it carried 800 liters of fuel. The three crew members had flown prior air races and the two pilots came in second in the 1981 Transatlantic Race.

GIUSEPPE DEMARIE was the commander of an airbus for Alitalia and had flown over 10,000 hours.

SAVINO BALZANO, the copilot, was the director of a company and a private pilot.

GIGLIOLA SCORTA, the photojournalist, was also a private pilot and had previously flown in several international rallies and three world championships.

The airplane's sponsor, CAFFÈ LAVAZZA, is a famous Italian coffee company that exports espresso to the US, Japan, Australia, and most European countries. It wanted to enter the Asian market.

CHRONOPOST – F-GGPM

This Cessna 210 Centurian was a single-engine aircraft with extra fuel tanks that gave it a range of eight hours. Chronopost, the race sponsor, was a new postal-messaging service and was responsible all through the competition for sending the films and reports of the professional reporters.

CLAUDE MAYNIÉ, the pilot, was a professional pilot and instructor at the national center of aviation training at Muret. He had flown in a previous air race and had flown to Chad for Médecins sans Frontières (Doctors Without Borders).

PATRICK GRANDPERRET was the copilot on the Paris-Beijing portion of the race. He was an engineer at the Direction Générale des Télécommunications and a private pilot. He had previously flown the Atlantic during Courrier Sud in 1985.

JORGE DE BRITO, also an engineer at the Centre de Recherche des Télécommunications Française and a private pilot, was the copilot on the return leg. He also had flown the Courrier Sud.

DOMINIQUE SIMON, a cameraman-photographer at the Ministry of Posts and Télécommunications, was the reporter on the outbound leg.

PIERRE PEYRICHOUT, the reporter on the inbound leg had worked for Radio France for many years and left to fly this air race.

ITALIA WINGS – F-GEIL

This twin-engine Cessna 310 was specially flown from the US for the race and was registered in France. It had several extra fuel tanks and an endurance of eleven hours. It was sponsored by Alimondo, a rapid transport agency, and by Max Meyer, the Italian leader in paint and floor coverings.

MAURO MASSON, the captain, was a professional pilot with Alitalia.

CLAUDIO SORO, the copilot, also was a pilot with Alitalia.

FRANCESCA OLDRINI was a journalist for the magazine *Panorama*. She also was a private pilot.

At the beginning of the race, it was unknown if they would be able to participate at all, as they had a problem getting their French-registered aircraft through Italian customs. They ultimately won the Beijing-to-Paris portion of the air race.

KOUROS YVES SAINT-LAURENT – F-BXAF

This twin-engine Cessna 310 was specifically bought for the race. It had extra fuel tanks that gave it an endurance of ten hours. The sponsor was Yves Saint-Laurent, and specifically Kouros perfumes.

RENAUD LAQUAY, the captain, was a professional pilot and Air France cabin staff head. He had participated in prior air races.

GASTON ROUSSAL (TONY) was a distributor of ties for Yves Sant-Laurent.

PIERRE FORSANS was the export director general of Yves Saint-Laurent perfumes.

LE BER–MASSON – F-GENR

This TB 20 Trinidad had an endurance of eight hours. The two pilots had previously competed in the Paris–New York–Paris race in 1981.

JEAN-MICHEL MASSON, the captain and a private pilot, was a psychiatrist and training director of special and aeronautical medicine at the Tours Medicine Faculty.

JEAN LE BER, the copilot, was a private pilot, an engineer at the European Space Agency in West Germany, and the head of the Meteosat data service.

MARIE DESNE was a journalist for the *Nouvelle République du Centre Ouest*.

The airplane was converted into a veritable mobile laboratory for the benefit of the European Space Agency. Jean was the guinea pig, carrying out a study program laid down by the German Institute of Spatial and Aeronautical Medicine. Covered with electrodes and equipped with a "halter" given to astronauts (an electro-cardiographic recorder), he captured all the cardiovascular consequences due to stress, fatigue, loss of sleep, and time offset. Every three hours, he would carefully record all the daily existence episodes.

LE HAVRE–NORMANDIE – F-BMLT

This Piper Comanche (PA 24) was the oldest machine and a collector's item. It was fitted with extra fuel tanks, which gave it an endurance of thirteen hours and thirty minutes. It was sponsored by several firms and organizations from the Haute-Normandy area.

MICHEL COGAN-PORTNOI, the aircraft commander, was a French doctor and private pilot.

YVES CRESSENT, the copilot, was an architect from Le Havre and a private pilot.

PIERRE GAILLARD, the reporter, also was a private pilot.

One of the sponsors was an art publishing firm, Phoebus, and a well-known painter, Daniel Authouart, who created two original works that were the official race pictures and would be presented to the head of state or high dignitary of each country visited. Our copies proudly hang in our home.

MANPOWER — F-GCQC

This twin-engine Cessna 310 had extra fuel tanks that gave it an endurance of twelve hours. It was the most beautiful airplane in the race, painted to resemble clouds in a blue sky. The sponsor, Manpower, is a world leader in temporary work.

DELIO IGLESIS, the captain, had been a professional aviator for at least twenty years, and it was said that he could decipher a flight plan before he could walk.

JEAN-CLAUDE DE LASSÉE, the copilot, was the president/director general of Assurances Universelles and Assurance des Investments Internationaux and a private pilot. Delio was his flight instructor.

STÉPHANE FRANCES was a reporter on TV Canal Plus.

Each member of this crew wore a striking one-piece silver flight suit.

MARTELL SPIRIT OF HONG KONG — F-GDHE

Cognac Martell, a famous French brandy, sponsored this twin-engine Cessna 335 with extra fuel tanks.

DAVID BEECHCROFT-KAY, the commander, was a captain on Cathay Pacific Airlines. He is the founder of an association that collects funds for Sunnyside, a school for handicapped children in Hong Kong.

KEVIN HOBAN, the copilot, was a flight engineer officer at Cathay Pacific and a flight instructor.

BONNIE ENGEL was the assistant chief editor of the magazine *Off Duty* in Hong Kong. She was a video specialist and already had made over 100 films for schools, private companies, and cable TV networks.

The Hong Kong crew, David and Kevin, were perfectionists. This crew, and particularly Bonnie, had the greatest sense of humor of any in the race. In Beijing, David presented a very advanced technique folding wheelchair to Deng Bu Fang, the son of Deng Xiaoping, who was handicapped himself and the president of the Association of Handicapped People in China.

MICROJET-MAMMOUTH – F-BSNO

This Wassmer 421 was one of the oldest and slowest of all of the airplanes. However, it had a range of sixteen and one-half hours, so no need to make time-consuming fuel stops. The sponsors were Hypermarché "Mammouth" and Marmande Aviation, the designer of Microjet, a little jet aircraft used for training fighter pilots.

RAYMOND MICHEL, a private pilot, was a former specialist of military radars and the owner of a hardware shop at Montargis.

CHRISTIAN LALOÉ, a copilot on an Air France 747, was the copilot outbound to Beijing.

RÉMY GRASSET, an engineer and glider instructor, was the copilot and reporter on the inbound leg. He was the winner of the African part of Courrier Sud in 1985.

JEAN-MARIE FRESNAULT, director of a data processing company at Montargis, was the reporter on the outbound leg. He came in second in the overall classification of the African part of Courrier Sud.

Raymond rebuilt the airplane for the race from a wreck. He and Jean-Marie spent many nights remaking the aircraft to get it into flying condition.

NOVASAM – F-GENO

This single-engine TB 20 Trinidad, with fuel giving it an endurance of nine hours, was sponsored by Novasam, a French firm dealing with temporary employment.

CLAUDINE SOBOL-OOSTERLINCK, a professional pilot and president of the French Women Pilots Association, was the captain.

JEAN KEMPNICH, a horticulturist and president of the Ailes Mosellanes's Aéroclub of Metz, was the copilot.

GILBERT MAYER, the reporter, was a journalist with the *Républican Lorrain* and a private pilot.

This was Claudine's first air race, but as a professional pilot, she already had a lot of international flying experience and frequently ferried aircraft across the pond to the US.

SPIRIT OF BRUSSELS – OO-AYZ

This Beechcraft Bonanza BE36 A with extra fuel tanks was financed by fifteen firms, including the Drouot Assurance Group, the Brussels region, Reynolds pens, TV-Ekspress, Overflight International, the Belgium Air Force, Petrofina, and the Holiday Inn hotel chain.

PATRICK SAILLEZ, a plastic surgeon, was the captain.

JEAN DE BROQUEVILLE, a professional pilot and pilot of Sabena, was copilot. He was the son and grandson of aviators.

DIDIER CLIPPE, a cameraman at R.T.L. TV, was the reporter.

Patrick had been a "flying doctor" in Tanzania and Kenya. Jean was his instructor. Jean was the grandson of the prime minister who, in 1927, had welcomed Charles Lindbergh to Brussels the day after his historic flight between New York and Paris. The crew carried a message in their baggage from Wilfried Martens, the Prime Minister of Belgium, to the Chinese people.

TDK – HB-PKP

The Piper Malibu PA 46 was the fastest of the single-engine airplanes with a top speed of 200 knots (370 mph). It was sponsored by Electro-Son, the exclusive importer and distributor in France of Japanese TDK products, such as audio and video cassettes.

FRANÇOIS GARÇON, the captain, was an Air France captain and an aéroclub instructor. At one time he had been the official pilot for the president of Burundi and had often helped Médecins sans Frontières (Doctors Without Borders) with their humanitarian missions.

PATRICK DUCOMMUN, the copilot, was Swiss and the owner of the aircraft and director of a transport company at Neufchâtel. He often flew WWII aircraft at rallies.

ALAIN THÉVENEAU, the photojournalist, was the director of a video production company and private pilot.

UMBERTO SALA – HB-LOT

The twin-engine PA 31 Navajo was equipped with extra fuel tanks giving it an endurance of nine hours.

BRUNO KEPPLER, the outbound captain, was a Swiss lawyer and private pilot with about 25,000 flying hours. He previously had taken part in the 1981 Transatlantic and 1984 Transafrican air races.

CLAUDE ALLEZ, the inbound captain, was the owner of a garage in Geneva. He was also a private pilot and had taken part in several other races.

LOUIS FRANCE, the outbound copilot, was a Swiss doctor and the director of a medical center in Geneva. He also participated in the 1981 and 1984 races.

NICOLAS PONCET, the inbound copilot, was the assets administrator for the Rothschild Bank of Geneva. He recently had become a pilot and had 400 flying hours.

JEAN-PIERRE MALIGNON, the photojournalist, was the director of a production house in Paris.

This all-Swiss crew was sponsored by Umberto Sala, the "Como Cravat King" who was responsible for the crews' clothing and decoration of the aircraft in the colors of a silk cravat inspired by the Italian flag. He had once created this tie to adorn the Leaning Tower of Pisa, which earned its place in the 1987 edition of the *Guinness Book of World Records*. He flew to each stopover in one of his organization's airplanes. He also gave one of his famous ties to each of the male race competitors.

VAIL SNAIL – N-4312V

This Piper Malibu PA 46 was the fastest of the single-engine Pipers.

CHUCK ROSENQUIST, the captain, was a real estate promoter and private pilot from Vail, Colorado, and was formerly an officer in the US Air Force. He was the owner of the airplane and was excited to include his family.

JEFF BENNET, the copilot, was an antique dealer in New York City and a professional pilot, accustomed to transatlantic ferrying.

TIMOTHY KNATCHBULL, the photojournalist, was a student with diplomas in sociology, politics, and psychology. He also was a private pilot, and the youngest pilot in the race. Two of his grandparents had been Viceroys of India: his paternal grandfather, the fifth Lord Brabourne, in 1937, and his maternal grandfather, Lord Mountbatten of Burma, from 1943 to 1945.

Chuck's wife, Peg, and two of his children, Christian and Eric, were passengers on the airplane. His daughter, Gretchen, joined them in Paris at the end of the race.

WINGED QUEST – N6113U

The Cessna 210 turbo Centurion, an unpressurized single-engine airplane, had extra fuel tanks giving it an endurance of eight hours.

JAMES BELL (JIM), the captain, is a lawyer and private pilot. He was a former officer in the US Air Force.

JUDITH LUND-BELL (JUDY), the copilot and Jim's wife, is also a lawyer and private pilot.

ALLEN FUNCH, the photojournalist, was the owner of a commercial shopping center.

This team, from Fresno, California, was accompanied by a plush giraffe, the mascot of Valley Children's Hospital in Fresno, and they used the race to raise money for the hospital. They were sponsored by many Fresno businesses. International English Institute had given them T-shirts to distribute as gifts, and the Raisin Wives of California gave them raisins, which were given mostly as gifts—though they ate some themselves.

Acknowledgments

To Bernard Lamy, the race director, his wife, Maryse, and their children, Patricia, Didier, and Bruno, who worked together tirelessly to plan and implement this historic event that forever changed our lives.

To Marc Mosier for being a real person and for convincing us to do something completely crazy.

To Reza, an internationally renowned photographer, the official race photographer and La Girafe's best friend who provided some of the photographs for this book in documenting this event.

We thank our sponsors who enabled us to experience this incredible month: Anne Speake, Annette Newman, Boots Camera, Capital Investors, Christiansen's Food World, Classic Car Wash, Dalton Moore, Don Monaco, Executive Wings, Inc., Fig Garden Village, G. L. Bruno, International English Institute, Michael Thielen, Patrick James, Paul Frederick, Penstar, Raisin Wives of California, Tom Richards, Tom and Carol Caswell, and Mayor Dale Doig.

We thank Stephanie Vasilovich who compiled a wonderful presentation for our sponsors. And Dalton Moore, the artist who designed the giraffe logo for us and helped with the brochure to obtain pledges for the trip to support the Valley Children's Hospital.

Sincere thanks to Executive Wings and Flint Aero mechanics who helped prepare the airplane for this adventure.

Annette Newman helped us obtain sponsors and threw a great party for us prior to our departure.

Our production team: Thanks to Pam Wallace, a wonderful longtime friend who guided and encouraged us throughout the process and who did the first rough edit. Rachael Bloom Krikorian gave us good advice and helped whenever we were at a loss as to what to do next. Barbara Noe Kennedy and Sandra Wendel, our thorough and responsive editors. Domini Dragoone, a talented artist and book production designer.

Last, but certainly not least: our children—Kevin, Edward, Karen, and Lisa—who were not only supportive but did not complain when we spent their inheritance.

About the Authors

Judy Lund-Bell and Jim Bell were both pilots and attorneys when they married in 1981. Both had been married previously, and each had two children ranging in age from twenty-three to twenty-seven at the time of the 1987 Paris-Pékin-Paris Air Race. Jim's son Kevin was the oldest, then Judy's son Edward, next Jim's daughter Karen, and the youngest, Judy's daughter Lisa.

When Jim and Judy married, all four children became "their" children, and Jim told Judy that if she became pregnant, he wanted a puppy. They have never had a dog, but once their neighbor's cat adopted them for a few years.

Jim is a business attorney and was a Certified Tax Specialist. Judy, also an attorney, was a Certified Family Law Specialist. She claims that Jim has the less-stressful practice, though he does not always agree. Their law practices are located in Fresno, California, where they have lived since 1966.

Prior to the race, Jim had been on various boards and was President of the board of Valley Children's Hospital and President of the Fresno County Bar Association. Jim's charitable contributions include being a board member of the Smittcamp Foundation and a founding board member of the Edward Lund Foundation, which was founded in 2015 after the death of their son, Edward, who died while pursuing his dreams and participating in a GranFondo bicycle race.

Judy had been a board member and officer and had donated time to many organizations, both legal, political, and charitable, including

Jim Bell and Judy Lund-Bell
(Judy is wearing the watch
she received from
King Hussein of Jordan).

Central California Legal Services and Centro La Familia, which provided low-cost legal services for the United Farm Workers and the Alternative Sentencing Program. She sat as Judge Pro Tempore and was a presenter of continuing education courses for the State Bar of California. Her political activism began in 1959 when she worked at John F. Kennedy's headquarters in Milwaukee, Wisconsin, while attending college there. She was a delegate for Hillary Clinton at the 2016 convention.

Judy was a board member of the Harbison Foundation and, as a gourmet cook, prepared French dinners to raise money for the San Joaquin River Parkway. She also participated in raising money for the scholarships awarded by the Edward Lund Foundation.

Jim and Judy both resigned from most of the boards they were on when they married in 1981, as they thought they would have no time for each other. Instead, they decided to have a date night every Wednesday evening. They still do.

After the race, Jim and Judy were both on the staff of the Aéroclub of France for the conference of the Federation Aéronautic International held in Toulouse in 1998.

Both of them had discovered a love of flying at an early age. Jim flew several times with a neighbor in Arkansas when he was very young. Judy watched airplanes take off and land from the Phoenix airport when she was in the sixth grade and wanted to fly away with them.

After college, Jim joined the Air Force hoping to fly. When he did not have that opportunity, he resigned, went to law school, and subsequently became a pilot. Judy completed law school as a single mother and then took flying lessons.

When they married, Jim already had the Cessna T210, tail number N6113U, and they flew it together around the United States and to the Bahamas and Mexico. But that was the limit of their international flying experience—until the air race. They both had their private pilot's license and an instrument rating. Jim also had a multi-engine and commercial rating and later obtained a turboprop rating as well.

After the air race, Judy obtained her multi-engine rating. They owned various airplanes throughout the years and eventually moved to Sierra Sky Park, located in the northwest part of Fresno, where every home has a hangar and residents can taxi on the wide streets to an airstrip in the center of the sky park.

Both Judy and Jim took many notes during the historic air race, and when they returned home, they neatly typed them and put them into a file cabinet. These pages did not formulate themselves into a book, so Judy decided that, after thirty-three years, it was time to give them some assistance. Thus, this book rises.

Made in the USA
Monee, IL
02 December 2020